P9-DBT-159

Usain Bolt

Usain Bolt

by George Cantor

LUCENT BOOKS

A part of Gale, Cengage Learning

GALE
CENGAGE Learning

Detroit • New York • San Francisco • New Haven, Conn • Waterville, Maine • London

GALE
CENGAGE Learning

LIBRARY OF CONGRESS CATALOGING-IN-PUBLICATION DATA

Cantor, George, 1941-
  Usain Bolt / by George Cantor.
    p. cm. -- (People in the news)
  Includes bibliographical references and index.
  ISBN 978-1-4205-0341-8 (hardcover)
  1. Bolt, Usain, 1986- 2. Track and field athletes--Jamaica--Biography.
  I. Title.
  GV1061.15.B66C36 2011
  796.42092--dc22
  [B]

2011006980

Lucent Books
27500 Drake Rd.
Farmington Hills, MI 48331

9 - 15

ISBN-13: 978-1-4205-0341-8
ISBN-10: 1-4205-0341-3

Printed in the United States of America
1 2 3 4 5 6 7 15 14 13 12 11

Printed by Bang Printing, Brainerd, MN, 1st Ptg., 06/2011

Contents

Fame and celebrity are alluring. People are drawn to those who walk in fame's spotlight, whether they are known for great accomplishments or for notorious deeds. The lives of the famous pique public interest and attract attention, perhaps because their experiences seem in some ways so different from, yet in other ways so similar to, our own.

Newspapers, magazines, and television regularly capitalize on this fascination with celebrity by running profiles of famous people. For example, television programs such as *Entertainment Tonight* devote all of their programming to stories about entertainment and entertainers. Magazines such as *People* fill their pages with stories of the private lives of famous people. Even newspapers, newsmagazines, and television news frequently delve into the lives of well-known personalities. Despite the number of articles and programs, few provide more than a superficial glimpse at their subjects.

Lucent's People in the News series offers young readers a deeper look into the lives of today's newsmakers, the influences that have shaped them, and the impact they have had in their fields of endeavor and on other people's lives. The subjects of the series hail from many disciplines and walks of life. They include authors, musicians, athletes, political leaders, entertainers, entrepreneurs, and others who have made a mark on modern life and who, in many cases, will continue to do so for years to come.

These biographies are more than factual chronicles. Each book emphasizes the contributions, accomplishments, or deeds that have brought fame or notoriety to the individual and shows how that person has influenced modern life. Authors portray their subjects in a realistic, unsentimental light. For example, Bill Gates—the cofounder and chief executive officer of the software giant Microsoft—has been instrumental in making personal computers the most vital tool of the modern age. Few dispute his business savvy, his perseverance, or his technical expertise, yet critics say he is ruthless in his dealings with competitors and driven more by his desire to maintain Microsoft's dominance in the computer industry than by an interest in furthering technology.

In these books, young readers will encounter inspiring stories about real people who achieved success despite enormous obstacles. Oprah Winfrey—the most powerful, most watched, and wealthiest woman on television today—spent the first six years of her life in the care of her grandparents while her unwed mother sought work and a better life elsewhere. Her adolescence was colored by rape, pregnancy at age fourteen, and sexual abuse.

Each author documents and supports his or her work with an array of primary and secondary source quotations taken from diaries, letters, speeches, and interviews. All quotes are footnoted to show readers exactly how and where biographers derive their information and provide guidance for further research. The quotations enliven the text by giving readers eyewitness views of the life and accomplishments of each person covered in the People in the News series.

In addition, each book in the series includes photographs, annotated bibliographies, timelines, and comprehensive indexes. For both the casual reader and the student researcher, the People in the News series offers insight into the lives of today's newsmakers—people who shape the way we live, work, and play in the modern age.

The Happy Sprinter

Of all of the various sports contests and activities, the purest might be running. What could be more directly athletic than the all-out dash, running as fast as you can to beat someone else?

True, in world-level competition techniques, strategies, equipment, training methods, track conditions, and even money and politics are involved. Yet, at its essence, the sport of sprinting is ultimately simple. Unlike in most other sports, there is no defense opposing the offense. The finish line is right there in sight, and each athlete is faced with the same task. Runners compete without regard to what a teammate might do, or fail to do. Runners do not wait for the coach to call a play. They do not depend on a referee or other official to award points. Runners just run, and the fastest person wins.

Early in the twenty-first century, into this pure sport came the pure spirit of Usain Bolt. This young Jamaican went from being simply a naturally fast kid to gaining global fame as a world champion in what seemed like a flash. Of course there was actually much more to the story.

The Difficulties

The hurdles that Bolt faced as a runner might not have been standing there on the track, but there were challenges nonetheless. He was born with a spinal condition. He grew up in a small, poor country. He was too tall for the sport, experts said. He did not seem serious enough about training. The training facilities in his country were inadequate compared to those in the United States, Canada, and Europe. He had injuries. He was a teenager who left the comfort of home to run against tough, experienced competitors in unfamiliar countries. Skeptics assumed he was using illegal performance-enhancing drugs. He partied a lot and laughed a lot. On the track, in important meets, he struck poses and showed off dance steps.

Nevertheless, by age twenty-three this same Usain Bolt had outrun everyone—everyone currently competing and everyone who had ever recorded a time in sprint competition. Bolt beat world records by unheard-of margins and finished so far ahead of rivals that they were not even in the picture at the finish line. Even more impressive, Bolt's best performances came in the highest-pressure venues: the World Championships and the Olympics.

Despite achieving such superiority, despite the global fame and torrent of money he gained at such a young age, Bolt remains courteous to all and supportive toward fellow athletes and young people in Jamaica and elsewhere. His relaxed lifestyle continues. Though it is sometimes hard to pursue an ordinary life while being followed by adoring crowds in Jamaica, Bolt has not changed much. He still parties, though not to excess. "He arrives at the club at two in the morning and leaves at five, so it's not like 10 hours' wild partying or anything,"[1] says his manager and mentor Norman Peart. He still spends his free time hanging out with old friends and playing video games and eating chicken nuggets.

Building Success

Bolt's easy-going attitude sometimes conceals the drive within him. It is, however, the shaping of his inner ambition that moved him from a sometimes awkward childhood to become an efficiently powerful champion. As a boy, his first sports love was cricket, not track. Then, with encouragement and coaching, he decided to take advantage of his natural speed. At first, being taller than other sprinters, he specialized in the two hundred-meter dash rather than the one hundred. Taller runners generally

Usain Bolt went from being a boy with a spinal condition to the fastest human in the world.

take longer to go from the standing start to full speed, and the longer distance suited Bolt's longer strides.

As he rose in the running ranks from national prominence to international meets, Bolt worked on improving his technique, especially for the starts. He knew well that the hundred-meter track event draws by far the most attention. To fulfill his championship desires, Bolt was determined to excel in the one hundred as well as the two hundred.

Among those standing in his way was one of Bolt's idols and countrymen, Asafa Powell. Though just a few years older than Bolt, Powell was already an established record breaker. Equally tough as Powell, both mentally and physically, was American sprinter Tyson Gay. Bolt had to overcome his awe of these other runners and convince himself he was in the same league with the intimidating Powell and Gay. By the start of the 2008 Olympics in Beijing, China, Bolt felt ready.

After the Olympics there was no doubt at all. With record-shattering performances in the one-hundred- and two-hundred-meter contests as well as the four-hundred-meter relay, Bolt became one of the most famous athletes in the world virtually overnight. His signature pose after winning a race of an archer letting an arrow fly represented the pure joy of Bolt the sprinter.

Perseverance

Practically as soon as Bolt crossed the finish line, skeptics began picking away at that joy. Some have accused him of showboating, noting that Bolt sometimes slowed down at the end of his races and gestured about the lack of competition. Worse, some insisted that no one could run as fast as Bolt without artificial enhancement; that is, steroids. Although everyone involved strongly denied Bolt was doping, there was in fact a previous connection between world-class sprinters and drug use. Jamaican-born Ben Johnson, who ran for Canada, was disqualified after a record-setting run in the 1988 Olympics, and the next two men who ran faster than 9.8 seconds in the hundred meters also failed their drug tests.

To dispel the rumors, Bolt continues to undergo frequent testing—thirty to forty times a year—and no problems have turned up. In Jamaica the allegations of drug use were regarded as biased and insulting toward the entire country. Bolt remained outwardly upbeat, cordial—and victorious. In 2009 at the World Championships, he surpassed his own stunning Olympic performances.

He continues volunteering to inspire others as well. In one of many examples, he agreed in 2010 to become a Youth Olympic Games ambassador, encouraging young people around the globe to become more active in sports. "I know how important it is to have mentors and role models when you are young to help give you focus and dreams to aspire to,"[2] Bolt says. His dedication was affirmed by someone who just two years before had been a severe critic of Bolt's so-called showboating. International Olympic Committee president Jacques Rogge declared that "children around the world look up to Usain and it is wonderful that he has decided to motivate young people to become more active."[3]

Chapter 1

A Surprising Beginning

The north coast of the Caribbean island nation of Jamaica is known for sugar plantations and spectacular scenery. This beautiful area has also become famous for speed, producing world-class runners who shatter records in international competitions.

The fastest of them all, Usain Bolt, was born in the tiny village of Sherwood Content, in the parish of Trelawny, on August 21, 1986, to Jennifer and Wellesley Bolt, who operated a small grocery store. Sherwood Content is in the hilly interior of Jamaica. It is a peaceful, rural village with no streetlights, a place where everyone knows everyone else and no one locks their doors. It took Bolt's accomplishments at the Olympics to bring the village some modern conveniences. "Usain's three gold medals brought us running water," said an elderly woman of the village. "Now we are praying for another gold medal to fix up the road."[4]

Usain, the youngest of three children, after a brother and a sister, was born a week and a half late, "the only time in his life he was slow,"[5] his mother says. He was born with scoliosis, a curvature of the spine that later contributed to a series of injuries that disrupted the runner's athletic progress. Even so, any slowness soon disappeared. His mother remembers he showed unusual strength at an early age: "He was very strong. At three weeks old he fell off the bed when I had left the room, and by the time I got back he was pushing himself around the place. It was from there that we noticed he was hyperactive."[6]

Usain's energy reached the point that his parents took him to a doctor. According to Usain's father, "The doctor reassured me that he was just hyperactive and I should be careful with him by the road."[7]

Quickness and Cricket

In fact, it was a fast neighborhood. Ben Johnson and Veronica Campbell-Brown, who went on to become Olympic sprinters, grew up just a few miles away. Wellesley Bolt had a theory about why his son and neighbors were so ready to run among the world's best. He said the yellow yams that area of Jamaica is known for gave them an edge. The potato-like yellow yams, which apparently originated in Africa, are served boiled or fried. They made up Usain's daily breakfast, along with dumplings and a green banana.

Usain Bolt's mother, Jennifer, stands in front of his childhood home in Sherwood Content, Jamaica.

Even in grade school, Usain was recognized as a special athlete fast enough to win the one-hundred-meter run in unofficial meets. But track was not the sport he liked best. Instead, his passion was cricket, one of the slowest-moving of all games, where competitions last entire days instead of seconds.

Cricket is a bat-and-ball game, a little like baseball, and is popular in England and in many former colonies of the British Empire—such as Jamaica. The rules are fairly complicated, but basically two teams of eleven play against each other on a round or oval field. The teams take turns batting and fielding. The main activity takes place in a rectangular space, called the pitch, outlined in the center of the oval. Inside the pitch and at opposite ends stand two wickets. The wickets consist of three posts about 28 inches (71cm) high that are connected by a horizontal piece

Bolt's father, Wellesley, looks through the window of his grocery store.

Cricket, a bat-and-ball game a little like baseball, is popular in Great Britain and its former colonies. Bolt excelled at the game while growing up.

across the top. A bowler (from the fielding team, who functions like a pitcher in baseball) stands in front of the wicket at one end of the pitch. One runner (from the batting team) stands beside the bowler. Another runner, also called a striker, stands at the opposite end of the pitch, in front of the opposite wicket. The bowler throws the ball toward the striker. The striker's job is to prevent the ball from hitting the wicket behind him and also to hit the ball into the field with his bat. When the striker hits the ball, he and the other runner run to the opposite ends of the pitch, to score a point. While the runners are running, the fielders try to get them out by catching the ball and throwing it at either one of the wickets, to knock it down before the runners reach the ends of the pitch. If the wicket is knocked down before the runners cross lines at the ends of the pitch (called creases), they are out.

Usain and his brother, Sadeeki, played cricket at every opportunity. Using an orange for a ball and a banana tree stump for the wicket, they would play in the road in front of their house. Usain decorated his bedroom walls with photographs of famous Jamaican and British cricket stars. When he entered William Knibb Memorial High School, however, even his cricket coach could see that it was the wrong game for him. "I'd look at that stopwatch as he ran up to bowl and think, 'There's something wrong with this watch,'" said coach Dwight Barnett. "'No kid can run that quickly.'"[8]

A New Direction

Barnett was friends with a great Jamaican athlete, sprinter Pablo McNeil, who had competed in the one-hundred-meter dash in the 1964 and 1968 Olympics. McNeil watched Usain work out, with that distance-eating stride, and knew he was seeing something special. Together the two coaches insisted that Usain give track a try. McNeil recalled his early efforts to make Usain a sprinter: "He was so stubborn. . . . But you didn't have to be a prophet to know that he was going to break world records."[9]

Barnett struggled to find ways to motivate his young athlete in the sport of track. Recalling that a mechanical rabbit is used to make greyhounds race on a track, Barnett thought Usain would respond to the challenge of chasing other runners. Barnett would line up his slower sprinters, give them a head start, and tell Usain to chase them down.[10]

The head of sports at the high school, Lorna Thorpe, became so close with Usain that she was called his second mother. Recognizing his unusual talents, she made sure he had what he needed to compete—including his first pair of track shoes, which she bought for him. Most importantly, however, she motivated him to excel, even if it required a little manipulation on her part: "I always thought it was my responsibility to get Usain to do his training. So I cried sometimes when he didn't do it and Mr. MacDonald, the maths teacher, would say to him, 'You've caused the staff to cry.' And he'd then immediately go and change for training."[11]

Little Country, Big Achievements

One of the great mysteries of international track competition is how the island of Jamaica, with a population smaller than that of the city of Chicago, Illinois, keeps turning out sprinters who grab the gold against competitors from much larger nations. Usain Bolt is part of a tradition that reaches back more than sixty years, to the first time Jamaica ever competed in the Olympics.

In those 1948 games, Jamaica's four-hundred-meter relay team shattered the world record. The team won again at the 1952 Olympics. Led by Herb McKenley and George Rhoden, the performance vaulted Jamaica into the forefront of Olympic achievement, turned the runners into national heroes, and made the sprint events the pride of the island.

Great runners such as Donald Quarrie and Merlene Ottey, who won medals in four different Olympics, became great coaches. That helped, in turn, to stop the outflow of promising young athletes to other countries, such as Canada and Britain, to train and kept them running under the Jamaican flag.

One of the biggest reasons for ongoing success has been that more Jamaican athletes are attending high school. In 1948 only an estimated 10 percent of eligible students were

enrolled in school. After 2000 the figure was closer to 95 percent, which means a greater pool of talent, incentives for better coaching, hopes for a better life after athletic competition is over, and a proud tradition.

Jamaica's men's four-hundred-meter relay team shattered the world record at the 1948 Olympic Games. The team won again in 1952.

Usain's First Big Test

McNeil decided that Usain's best event was the two-hundred-meter run. Unlike the one hundred meters, it is not an all-out dash. The longer length—about 1/8 of a mile (0.2km)—seemed better suited to Usain, giving him time to get into his longer stride and catch shorter opponents. McNeil entered Usain in Champs, Jamaica's all-island high school track championship, in 1999. Track in Jamaica is as popular as football is in the United States. It is not unusual for thirty thousand spectators to attend a Champs meet. It is a flag-waving, band-blasting event, and articles about the winners appear on the news pages as well as the sports pages of the local newspapers.

Any young Jamaican with the slightest spark of talent competes in Champs, and very few of them advance any further. As many as three thousand boys and girls enter the meet each year. The competition is keen, and the training is grueling. Talent alone is not enough to impress coaches and trainers. They are looking for more, and that includes the inner fire it takes to achieve the ultimate reductions in time and the mental toughness to overcome the distractions that get in the way. In his first Champs competition, the tall, skinny, thirteen-year-old runner from Trelawny did not impress the experts. He reached the finals, but did not win a medal.

Many doubted that Usain, with his upbeat personality, had the kind of focus necessary to become a champion. His natural talent was so great, however, that in just two more years, by the time he was fifteen, he had won the silver medal in the two-hundred-meter run at Champs and was ready for wider competition. He took two more silver medals at an all-Caribbean event and just missed the finals at the 2001 World Youth Championships in Hungary.

Also, when Usain was fifteen, Lorna Thorpe introduced him to a tax auditor, Norman Peart. Peart, then twenty-eight years old, had been an athlete at the same high school that Usain attended before going on to college and a business career. The two hit it off, and Peart became Usain's manager and soon afterward one of his most trusted advisers. Peart later described his role: "You have to have someone who has your back. He [Usain] says I tell him he's spending too much. But he needs someone around him to tell him like it is, to say: 'Hey, you're doing crap.' Successful people have friends who hang around and only say, 'Hey everything's fine.'"[12]

Peart set out to build a small but effective structure for Usain, and his influence wound up reaching all aspects of Usain's life. As time went on, Peart became involved in Usain's training, education, motivation, and physical conditioning—in particular, addressing the problems caused by his scoliosis. The affliction

Bobsledding Is Serious

At first, people thought it was a joke. Why would Jamaica, a sunswept Caribbean island with a tradition of producing champion sprinters, enter the 1988 Winter Olympics with a bobsled team? It seemed absurd, and more than a few European teams were angry because they thought Jamaica was mocking their sport. But they were wrong.

Jamaican coaches understood that the same leg strength and bursts of speed essential to running sprints could be applied to bobsledding. Moreover, eager young Jamaicans who did not have quite the ability of a Usain Bolt in track might find an outlet for their talent on the icy bobsled track.

It took some convincing, but four members of the Jamaican army agreed to try the sport. They spent hours practicing on a flat cement surface with a battered sled. Against all expectations they actually made it to the third heat of the four-round competition at the Olympics in Calgary before crashing.

Their effort was so courageous that they won over those who had sneered at them only a few days before. The team competed in several more Olympics and went on to finish fourteenth in the thirty-sled field in 1994. The story of the first Jamaican bobsled team is told in the 1993 movie *Cool Runnings*.

is essentially of unknown cause. There is no known cure, either, but various treatments can diminish its effects.

The Young New Star

Another event, the World Junior Championships, was held in Kingston, the capital of Jamaica, in 2002, and that was where Usain broke through in spectacular fashion. Still one month shy of his sixteenth birthday, he became the youngest athlete ever to win gold in the two hundred meters. His time of 20.65 seconds was a record for the event. Then he added two silvers, in the one-hundred-meter sprint and in the four-hundred-meter relay. Suddenly, he was one of the biggest names in Jamaican sports, a track superstar while still in high school.

"He had three medals clinking around his neck when anyone else was lucky to just have one," says Germaine Mason, a high jumper on the Jamaican team. "There he was, walking along, joking with everybody, clink, clink, clink."[13]

With the fame came pressure, however. It was customary for promising Jamaican athletes to be sent abroad, to countries where coaching and training facilities were supposedly better. But Usain's accomplishments were so stunning that the possibility of his leaving Jamaica became a political issue. P.J. Patterson, the prime minister of Jamaica, wanted the young track star to stay in the country to train, so he moved Usain to Kingston with government support. Peart had earned the trust of Usain's parents, who allowed their son to live with him in Kingston. "He was still a kid," Peart said. "I go out of my way with him, always, because of that. There is trust. His parents call me 'Mr. Peart,' even though his dad is old enough to be my dad."[14]

Drawn by Bright Lights

The move was a bit overwhelming for a young man from a country village. Kingston is a lively place, with plenty of opportunities for behavior that is not helpful for someone intent on serious athletic training. Elton Tucker, an editor with the *Kingston Gleaner*, the country's largest newspaper, painted this

Bolt celebrates his record-breaking two-hundred-meter race victory at the 2002 World Junior Championships in Jamaica. He became the youngest athlete ever to win a gold medal in the two hundred meters.

picture of Usain at the time: "He liked the nightclubs, . . . and he thought he could run on natural talent alone."[15]

The bright lights of the big city distracted Usain from his training, and Jamaican officials took notice. When it came time to select runners for the Senior Championships in Paris, France, they left him off the roster because they felt he had not shown enough maturity to compete at that level. It was a blow to Usain's pride, and for the first time he began to examine his priorities and to question what he was doing.

Asafa Powell, four years older than Usain, was then Jamaica's reigning track hero. He was a superstar who could drive around Kingston in either his BMW or his Mercedes. Usain had grown up in a poor family and realized that track could be his ticket to a better life, just as it was for Powell. When Usain lost his place on the senior team, it came as a shock and provided a wake-up call for the young athlete. From that point on, Usain rededicated himself to becoming a world-class athlete like Powell.

Chapter 2

The Rivals

Young men in Jamaica who are intent on following a career in track soon learn that they are racing not only against the clock, but also against powerful rivals, runners from the past and present, whose records resonate in their minds.

Bolt's sense of his place and his potential in the world of track soon became apparent to him. When he combined his enormous natural talent with his renewed dedication to training, he began to shatter records in both high school and international events. In 2003 he won gold in the two-hundred-meter competition in the World Youth Championships in Quebec, Canada. In the semifinals and the finals, Bolt displayed a habit that would become part of his racing signature: As he neared the finish line he looked to the side, saw no one close to beating him, and then almost coasted the last few meters. In the same year, Usain broke the Jamaican high school records for both the two-hundred-meter and four-hundred-meter events.

Bolt drew a lot of attention at track meets. He already had reached his adult height of 6 feet, 5 inches (1.95m), and track experts could not remember an athlete who was that tall excelling as a sprinter—especially one so young.

With so many wins and record-breaking times, Bolt had a decision to make: Was he ready to turn professional? Guided by his new coach, Fitz Coleman, Bolt concluded that it was time, and he took this big step in 2004 when he was just eighteen years old. Coleman entered him in the CARIFTA Games, an all-Caribbean track meet held in Bermuda and sponsored by the Caribbean Free Trade Association (CARIFTA), in the spring of

2004. It was Bolt's first professional appearance and regarded as a good warm-up for the upcoming Olympics in Athens, Greece. He won a gold medal in the CARIFTA Games, crossing the finish line in under twenty seconds in the two-hundred meters for the first time and shattering the world junior record for the event.

But the price was high. The young runner injured a hamstring—a tendon at the back of the knee—and as the calendar moved closer to the Olympics in Athens it was becoming apparent that he would not be at full strength for the competition there. The Jamaican Olympic Committee showed its confidence in him by keeping him on the roster for the two-hundred-meter

In his first professional race in 2004 at the CARIFTA Games, Bolt won the gold in the two hundred meters. He finished the race in under twenty seconds for the first time and shattered the world junior record.

run. But the injured leg did not hold up to the stress, and he was eliminated in the first round of trials.

It was a bitter disappointment for the young star. Yet his career was just beginning, and as his leg healed he was looking forward to his first full season on the professional running circuit. This was his chance to establish himself as a serious figure at the highest level of international competition.

A Tougher Coach

With that chance came another coaching change. The new coach, Glen Mills, was famous as a disciplinarian, a man who would not tolerate a runner slipping into sloppy training habits. When Mills was a teenager himself, he knew he had no running talent, but he was fascinated by track, and he hung around his high school's athletic department offices to help out. When he was thirteen, he managed to get himself appointed an assistant coach. When a new headmaster arrived at the school, however, Mills was removed from the coaching staff. The move proved so unpopular that most of the school's top runners trained with Mills off campus, so Mills was allowed to return to the staff.

By the early 1970s, Mills's reputation for nurturing young sprinters had grown across Jamaica. He became Jamaica's head coach for track in 1987, and under his direction Jamaican athletes went on to win thirty-three Olympic medals and seventy-one World Championship medals. Mills retired as national coach in 2009 but continued to work with Bolt.

All along, Mills had been watching the young Bolt's performance closely. When he felt that Bolt was essentially an adult and mature enough to accept the discipline Mills demanded, the pair teamed up, ready to emerge as a force to be reckoned with in the world of track. One thing in particular that Mills did was guide Bolt toward proper running techniques. He noted that Bolt was running behind his center of balance, a posture that stressed his hamstrings. Using slow-motion videos, Mills instructed Bolt on how to achieve just the right degree of forward lean while running at maximum velocity.

Glen Mills, pointing, became Bolt's coach in 2005 when he felt Bolt had matured enough to accept the discipline Mills demanded.

"We . . . turned Usain's size into a motor instead of a brake,"[16] explains Mills. With that final adjustment, Bolt at last was ready to put the years of doubt and frustration behind him and reach for the pinnacle of sprinting stardom.

Bolt entered the European track circuit in the spring of 2005, and at one meet after another his performance took him higher in the international rankings. He stunned British track experts by crashing through the sub-twenty-seconds barrier for the two-hundred-meter run in London, and by the end of the year he was ranked in the top five in the world for that event.

The 2005 World Championships were held in Helsinki, Finland, and once more it appeared that Bolt was going to dominate the field. Then bad luck and nagging injuries struck again. He qualified for the two-hundred-meter finals but then, hobbled with an injury, he finished dead last in the eight-man field, almost six seconds behind the seventh-place finisher. For the second year in a row, the top prize in his sport had been swept away from him, and he could only watch helplessly.

Was He Too Tall?

Mills began to fear that for all his gifts of speed and strength, Bolt might never be able to run an injury-free season. He already was being called "The Freak" because of his extraordinary height and lean frame. In fact, researchers decided Bolt's career would be brief. A 2005 study conducted by the *Journal of Sports Science and Medicine* concluded that 6 feet, 3 inches (1.9m)—2 inches (5cm) less than Bolt's height—was the absolute maximum for an effective sprinter. It declared that the explosive starts that sprinters make over and over again put too much strain on the legs and thighs of anyone taller. Injuries would therefore be unavoidable for Bolt.

Bolt works out during one of Mills's training sessions. Mills's adjustments moved Bolt's shoulders forward to be even with his center of gravity and shortened his stride to reduce the stress Bolt's height caused on his joints.

Olympic Broadcasting

When the modern Olympics were revived in 1896, there were many noble sentiments repeated about reaching international understanding through sports. But 112 years later, it was marketing and media coverage that dominated the games in Beijing, China. The final tally showed that around 4.7 billion TV viewers worldwide watched some part of those Olympics.

Moreover, an entirely new set of broadcast rights, including online streaming, was negotiated in a separate package. This segment of the market was growing nine times faster than traditional media outlets. Even so, copyright restrictions made the games less accessible than they might have been, and there still was no international coverage. Each national media outlet simply televised events that would be of interest to its own audience.

Those who visited the games were flooded with images of "Dancing Beijing," an emblem that symbolized a welcoming with open arms. The mascots, the five Fuwa, represented each of the Olympic rings as a symbol of Chinese culture. The slogan was "One World, One Dream," chosen from 210,000 entries from around the world.

Over 4.7 billion TV viewers tuned in worldwide to watch the 2008 Olympic Games in Beijing.

There had always been a wobble in Bolt's technique when he was a young sprinter. He lacked the muscular development to guide himself in a straight line as a fifteen-year-old. It did not stop him from breaking records in his age group, but his technique had to improve if he planned to compete and win at the professional level.

Mills had an idea. He decided to try reducing the stress that came with Bolt's height by shortening his long stride. Even the coach himself later admitted that such an approach sounded odd. But the adjustment moved Bolt's shoulders forward so that they were now even with his center of gravity and reduced the time his feet were not in contact with the running surface.

Something to Prove

Bolt finally began showing what he was capable of in 2006. He was in the top five internationally by the end of that year and ran a personal best of 19.88 seconds in the two hundred meters. After that, he continued to climb up the rating charts. He won a bronze medal at the World Athletics finals in Stuttgart, Germany, and then a silver medal at the World Cup in Athens.

Bolt also wanted to run the one hundred meters, the glamour event of track, but first, Mills told him, he had to concentrate more on his times in the two-hundred-meter event. So Bolt, with improved health as well as technique, ran the two hundred meters in the 2007 Jamaican Championships and beat the record set back in 1976 by legendary Jamaican track star Donald Quarrie. Bolt hit the finish line with a time of 19.75 seconds. Veteran track observers said that they had not seen anyone take the turn in the two hundred meters with such speed and grace since Quarrie retired.

Mills kept his promise and allowed Bolt to enter the one hundred meters at the Vardinoyiannia meeting in Crete, Greece later that year. In his first attempt, he won the gold medal. In the 2008 Jamaica Invitational he finished the one hundred in 9.76 seconds. It was the second-fastest time ever recorded in the event.

The Two to Beat

As Bolt dedicated himself to success in both the one-hundred-meter and two-hundred-meter events, he entered the realm of track's highest level. Traditionally, the greatest runners excelled in both events, able to blast through the shorter dash as well as sustain top speed through the longer sprint.

For Bolt, the records of two major rivals in particular stood out. Track stars Donald Quarrie and Asafa Powell were both national idols in Jamaica. Every time Bolt entered a meet, in essence he was running against these two—one as a legend, and the other often right there on the track with him.

In the almost forty years since Quarrie had run the one hundred and two hundred meters, he had become more than a national track star. He was a living legend, a Jamaican hero. When Bolt entered the stadium in Beijing for the 2008 Olympic Games, in his mind—and in the minds of Jamaicans—he was going up against the adored legend of Quarrie, who had become a superstar while in his teens. Quarrie had won three gold medals in the Montreal Commonwealth Games of 1970 at the age of nineteen. Songs were written about him. Quarrie followed that up with two more gold medals at the Commonwealth Games in 1974. His name became a household word, and people would say things like, "I was running so fast even Donald Quarrie couldn't catch me."

Quarrie became a national hero when he went on to win gold and silver medals at the 1976 Olympics, breaking world records in both the one hundred and two hundred meters. They were the first Olympic gold medals won by a Jamaican in twenty-four years, and Quarrie achieved a status equal to that of U.S. baseball hero Babe Ruth or basketball superstar Michael Jordan—the best there was or ever would be. Even decades later, the luster has not worn off. Quarrie's legacy is undeniable and unavoidable. A statue of the runner stands at the entrance to the National Stadium in Kingston. His accomplishments sparked a rebirth in Jamaican track and established a line of international competitors that led straight to another Jamaican track star, Asafa Powell.

Asafa Powell shows his world record time of 9.77 seconds in the one-hundred-meter race during the 2005 Athens Super Grand Prix games.

Then Came Powell

Powell's achievements also loomed over Bolt's aspirations. Another one of the "country boys," as the sportswriters in Kingston call runners from Jamaica's small towns, Powell was born in Spanish Town in 1982. His parents were both ministers, and he was the youngest of six children.

Powell specialized in the one hundred meters. He won his first international gold in 2004 when he was twenty-two years old and effectively cleared out all competition. "I'm running against myself," he said at the time. "I'm the only one who can defeat myself and I don't intend to."[17]

Powell presented a positive image off the track and was known for enjoying his collection of antique automobiles and sports cars. Even so, his family had been haunted by tragedy. In 2002, Powell's brother Michael was murdered in a New York

Sticking with Chicken

Usain Bolt decided to follow a very limited menu before his events at Beijing. It consisted of two portions of chicken nuggets every day.

"I wasn't sure," he says. "I decided—you know what—to focus on the nuggets because there's no messing there. I'll be more sure of the food in London in 2012" for the Olympics there.

Bolt's reluctance to sample a wider variety of one of the world's great national cuisines is understandable. Some of the menu translations would have frightened off anyone.

For example, there is Husband and Wife Lung Slice. It was actually pieces of pork lung in chili sauce. A Braised Lion's Head was stewed pork balls in a brown sauce. Strange Flavored Shredded Chicken turned out to be not so strange, but then there were French Beans in Coca-Cola.

Quoted in Donald McRae. "Usain Bolt Warns the World's Sprinters That the Best Is Yet to Come." *Guardian* (Manchester, UK), March 30, 2010, p. 6.

City taxi. Another brother, Vaughn, collapsed and died playing American football in Georgia the following year. Both brothers had passed away while Powell was at the Jamaican National Trials and Championship. But he struggled on and made both teams. Then his brother Donovan, also a runner, died of a heart attack in 2003.

Asafa Powell had been a favorite to win a medal at the 2004 Athens Olympics, but it was not to be. Powell finished a disappointing fifth in the finals for the one-hundred-meter run and then pulled out of the two-hundred-meter event, even though qualifying for it earlier.

The next year, in June, Powell returned to Athens and reasserted his top-rank status by setting the world record for the one hundred meters. He tore through the distance in 9.77 seconds. Then in the 2006 Commonwealth Games in Melbourne,

Australia, he won a gold medal in the hundred. Despite a rain-slicked track surface, Powell powered to a 9.87-second time, with the second-place finisher not even close. The following year, 2007, Powell beat his own world record with a new time of 9.74 seconds in the hundred.

Powell had established himself as a favorite for the 2008 Olympics. Bolt, despite his strength and a handful of spectacular results, remained overshadowed by Powell as well as by Quarrie's legacy.

Chapter 3

Olympic Showdown

For track fans, anticipation grew throughout the early months of 2008. Not only was this an Olympic year, but also an extraordinary set of sprinters aimed to settle just who was the fastest man on earth.

In early May 2008, running in the Jamaica International Invitational, the rising star Usain Bolt fell just 0.02 seconds short of Jamaican rival Asafa Powell's one-hundred-meter record. When Bolt shattered the mark four weeks later in the New York Grand Prix, it was just his fourth race at that distance in major competition. Bolt won a gold medal and broke Powell's record by 0.02 seconds, with a time of 9.72 seconds. Still, Bolt was considered more of a curiosity than a pre-Olympic favorite, with his history of injuries and his too-tall "freak" image.

It was Powell rather than Bolt who was regarded as the top sprinter in Jamaica as the athletes planned for the Beijing Olympics in 2008. And Powell came across as having the properly competitive attitude about being on the world's brightest athletic stage. "It doesn't scare me," Powell said. "The guys I am running against in Beijing are the same ones I run against all year. It's no different at the Olympics—it's just a name and you should put it aside until you cross the line."[18]

Clearly, both men were heading to China with something to prove. Bolt, though, had the greater burden. He had yet to achieve the long record of competitive success set by his teammate/rival. Powell refused to get into a trash-talking match with

Bolt, in which rivals put down their opponents in public in order to stir up interest in the upcoming event. "We've been friends too long for that," he said. "I knew my heart wouldn't be in it."[19] Yet his heart was also telling him that Bolt was the one he had to beat.

For Bolt, it did not matter that he had already eclipsed Powell's record, at least once. It also did not matter that Powell had sustained a series of frustrating injuries during the first half of 2008. Bolt was keenly aware that his close friend would be his main rival in Beijing. The fact was that only when the two competed directly for the biggest prizes in track, under the greatest pressure, the matter would be resolved.

Still, it was a friendly rivalry. Even as their prominence grew, little had changed between them "except that Usain is getting to be a lot more famous," said Powell. "A rivalry is something this sport hasn't seen in a good long while. But all I need to do is run my own race to beat him."[20]

In the 2008 New York Grand Prix, Bolt broke the one-hundred-meter world record with a 9.72 time. It was only his fourth race at that distance.

The U.S. Star

There was a third runner in this equation. He was an American, Tyson Gay, who led the University of Arkansas to consecutive college championships in 2004 and 2005 while winning the one-hundred-meter title. He was fast from the outset, showing his talent early in baseball. "I could steal a few bases," Gay said. "But I never could beat my sister. She was a year older than me and had a head start. But she also inspired me."[21]

In 2006, Gay's first year as a professional, he took a silver medal in the two hundred meters and a gold in the World Athletics final

Blazing Glory

With his triple gold performances in 2008, Usain Bolt was following a star-studded path. The sprinters have always been the glamour athletes of the Olympics. Any listing of great Olympic moments would have to include several sprinters.

The best known is probably Jesse Owens, who won four gold medals in the highly politicized 1936 games in Berlin in Nazi Germany. German dictator Adolf Hitler had proclaimed the physical superiority of Aryan, or white non-Jewish, males. Therefore, Hitler chose to leave the stadium in a fury rather than watch Owens, an African American, and his teammates defeat the Germans and prove Hitler's theories wrong.

Owens tied the Olympic record for the one hundred meters with a time of 10.3 seconds. In the two hundred meters he set a record in the first heat and then bettered that with a time of 20.7 seconds in the final. He then ran with Ralph Metcalfe, Foy Draper, and Frank Wykoff as they took the 4x100 meters with a world record of 398 seconds. (The only two Jewish members of the team were withdrawn from competition to soothe Nazi outrage.) Owens's fourth gold was in the long jump.

Movie fans know about Olympic sprinters from the film *Chariots of Fire*, which details the heroic performance of the 1920 British team at the Antwerp, Belgium, games.

in Monte Carlo. Gay soon became the greatest threat to the dominance of Powell in men's track. Throughout 2006 he racked up two more first-place finishes, then topped it off in 2007 with gold medals in the one hundred, the two hundred, and the four-man relay at the World Championships in Osaka, Japan, where his competition included Powell and Bolt. By the start of the Olympic year Gay was rated as an even bet with Powell. Gay describes his approach to competition: "I am a religious man, so I really believe in my God-given ability that I can do the unexpected. I really do believe I can break a record or win a medal. When I see guys like [sprinter] Michael Johnson, and I've run some of the same times they have, it's just shocking. That victory lap in Osaka is one I'll never forget."[22]

Bolt on the Rise

Then Bolt really began to come on strong. In two direct meetings with Gay in 2008, Bolt defeated him handily. "It looked as though his knees were going past my face,"[23] said a dejected Gay. It was an important psychological breakthrough, and Bolt's world record run in New York came less than a month later.

Powell, however, was not intimidated. "I've made a lot of improvements over the last year, worked on the start more and worked on the finish," he said in June 2008. He was still feeling the effects of an ankle injury sustained in April, "which is not going to get any worse, so why not compete on it? I'm definitely not quite a 10 in shape and I'm just trying to keep it loose."[24]

Powell had the benefit of far more extensive Olympics experience than the then-injured Bolt obtained at the 2004 Athens, Greece, games. Gay also was trying to fight his way through a groin injury; since his two defeats by Bolt his standing had fallen off dramatically. He still held the international mark of 19.58 in the two hundred meters and had set a U.S. record for the hundred-meter run with 9.77 seconds. So he could not be ignored. Commentators insisted, however, that the Gay who would run at Beijing was, as one put it, "not really Tyson Gay."[25]

U.S. runner Tyson Gay, left, congratulates Bolt after he defeated Gay in the one hundred meters at the Reebok Grand Prix on May 31, 2008. Gay said of Bolt "It looked as if his knees were going past my face."

So as August rolled around, the stage was set in Beijing, China, for one of the greatest confrontations in recent track history.

It had taken years for Bolt to fight through injuries and mental disappointments before nearing the pinnacle of his sport. Setting the new record for the hundred meters had come just three months before the Olympics opening ceremony. That performance in New York had made Bolt a household name in those countries where track has a large fan base and gets a lot of coverage in the media. Now fans could buy T-shirts and watches with Bolt's face on them. The possibility that this young man just

might be one of the greatest runners in history first began to be discussed. Powell's coach, Stephen Francis, commented, "Every once in a while people come along in the world who are exceptional. You have [Albert] Einstein. You have Isaac Newton. You have [Ludwig van] Beethoven . . . and you have Usain Bolt."[26]

He Makes It Look Easy

The official Olympics website described Bolt as coming out of "relative obscurity" before he shattered the one-hundred-meter record. He not only lowered the record, he left the impression that he could have done even better before seeming to coast with about fifteen meters left in the race.

Some commentators called that arrogance. Others simply saw it as the exuberant joy of a top athlete reaching peak form and realizing no one else on the track had a chance of beating him. Somehow, it seemed, he was a big kid who had been touched by magic.

When he arrived in Beijing for the start of the Olympics, Bolt even claimed to be only 80 percent sure that he would enter both the one-hundred- and two-hundred-meter events. "I leave those decisions to my coach,"[27] he said. In fact, his coach, Glen Mills, already had announced he would definitely enter both, Bolt was reminded. "That's the first time I am hearing that," said Bolt, with a huge smile. "It must have been a miscommunication between us."[28]

But everyone in the interview room could tell that Bolt welcomed the challenge and recognized that these would be the defining races of his career.

"There is no magic," he insisted. "It all comes down to hard work, dedication and a competitive spirit for us Jamaicans, and we are like that in other aspects of life, too."[29]

A Two-Part Challenge

No one had won both the one hundred and two hundred in the same Olympics since American Carl Lewis in Los Angeles in 1984. Bolt also was fully aware that he would walk onto the track

Cheers and Boos

Half a century after the Berlin games, another powerful American athlete, Carl Lewis, duplicated Jesse Owens's achievement on the field—but Lewis was not hailed as a hero in the same way.

In the 1984 Olympics in Los Angeles, Lewis took the one hundred meters in 9.99 seconds despite a slow start, pulling away with twenty meters to go. He broke a record in winning the two hundred meters with a time of 19.80 seconds, and then he ran an 8.94-second anchor leg to victory in the 4x100 relay as the team set another record. In addition, like Owens, Lewis won the long jump gold medal.

Lewis, however, struck many as purely self-advancing. During the games he did not stay at the Olympic Village with other athletes. His personal manager said he wanted Lewis to become as rich as singer Michael Jackson. When he ran his one-hundred-meter victory lap holding an American flag handed to him by a fan, critics charged (without foundation) that Lewis had planted the fan and flag.

At the 1984 Los Angeles Olympic Games American Carl Lewis repeated Jesse Owens's feat of winning four gold medals.

with the former world record holder, Asafa Powell, and current world champion, Tyson Gay. "Asafa even thanked me for taking some of the pressure off him," Bolt said. "We are good friends and proud Jamaicans but on the track we have to run for ourselves."[30]

Bolt had been considered at the age of seventeen as a strong contender in the two hundred meters during the 2004 Athens Olympics. But a devastating hamstring injury had eliminated him in the first round of heats, and Bolt said afterward that if it had not been the Olympics he would not have run at all.

Throughout the following two years a series of back and knee injuries kept him on the sidelines, including during the 2005 World Championships in Helsinki, Finland. Bolt shrugged the injuries off as the price of becoming a champion. "I have learned a lot and it forces you to grow up quickly," he said. "I am hungry for a title under my belt, so you have to be serious, buckle down and do the work required."[31]

His training regimen went year round; five times a week on the track and three times in the gym. "When I even think of easing off my training I think about my parents," Bolt said. "They took care of me when I was a child and now I want to take care of them and keep them smiling."[32] Indeed, after Bolt surpassed Donald Quarrie's record in the two hundred meters in the summer of 2007, nasty rumors about halfhearted training stopped.

Above All Others

Remi Korchemny, a track coach from the former Soviet Union, said that Bolt was the finest physical specimen the track world had ever seen:

> Running consists of three components: stride length, air time and ground time. It depends on explosiveness, how fast athletes can replace their limbs from one point to another and with exactly the proper angle and the proper reaction in the proper time.

> He reaches his maximum velocity a little bit later than other runners because his stride length is longer. But once he reaches it, no one has the same kind of explosiveness.[33]

Bolt also towered over other sprinters. So some commentators compared him to America's top basketball players. Charlie Greene, longtime college track coach and world-record holder in the one hundred meters in the late 1960s, made this comparison: "Maybe some of them could be on the same level as Bolt or Asafa Powell. [basketball stars] LeBron James. Michael Jordan. Both of them have that kind of quickness and speed, but they preferred making money in another activity. In America it is impossible for athletes of that size to train for track."[34]

The Buzz Begins

On August 15, 2008, it was finally time to let the big games begin. In Beijing, when Bolt prepared to step onto the track for the first heat of the one hundred meters, observers said an audible buzz filled the main stadium, known as the Bird's Nest. Bolt ran an astonishing 9.92 for the heat, while apparently jogging the last fifteen meters.

Veteran track commentators such as Donovan Bailey, the 1996 gold-medal winner, said they had never before seen a run like this in a preliminary heat for the one hundred meters. It was the easiest 9.92 seconds they had ever witnessed.

On the evening of the hundred-meter finals, the buzz around Bolt's potential had turned into a surge of electricity that could have illuminated a small town. Music filled the stadium, and Bolt seemed to be rocking to the beat before entering the starting blocks. He pointed to his country's name on his jersey. He shot off a make-believe arrow, a gesture Bolt said he had begun using to ease his homesickness as the track circuit took him far from Jamaica. He joked with a volunteer at the starting line. Six of the eight finalists in Beijing were from the Caribbean, the greatest number ever in an Olympics.

The runners crouched in their blocks. A gunshot sounded and a race against time and history had begun. After thirty meters, Bolt looked buried in the middle of the pack. But in a sudden burst of breathtaking speed he seemed to leave the rest of the field slogging through mud. Within five strides he was

Before winning his gold medal in Beijing, Bolt first demonstrated his gesture of shooting an arrow in the air. He claims he did it to ease his homesickness when he was far from Jamaica.

in the lead. Five more and he was uncatchable. It was calculated later that in each second he was covering twelve meters, or
about forty feet.

What really made observers aghast was the fact that Bolt
visibly slowed down near the finish line: In the midst of his
highest-pressure race ever, he looks to the side, sees no one
is challenging him, and stops pumping his arms hard. He almost glides to the finish line. The Institute of Theoretical As-
trophysics in Oslo, Norway, concluded that if Bolt had kept up
his pace to the end he would have finished in an other-worldly
time of 9.52 seconds. As it was, his new world record was 9.69
seconds.

Runner-up Richard Thompson, of Trinidad and Tobago, finished 0.2 seconds behind, giving Bolt the widest victory margin
in the event in twenty-four years. "He is a phenomenal athlete,"
said Thompson. "It was only a matter of time before he started
producing what he is producing now."[35]

Criticism and Celebration

What got the world media chattering, though, was Bolt's apparent coasting at the end. Some athletes were deeply offended
and called it "showboating." Jacques Rogge, president of the International Olympic Committee, condemned Bolt's action and
called him disrespectful. A few others also pointed out that one
of his shoelaces seemed to be untied.

But Bolt saw it another way. "I just blew my mind. I blew
the world's mind and I wasn't bragging," he said. "When I saw
I wasn't covered, I was just happy."[36] Right after the race Bolt
further expressed his joy by doing a Jamaican dance known as
the gully creeper. The Jamaican government minister of sport,
Edmund Bartlett, defended him: "We have to see it in the glory
of their moment. We have to allow the personality of youth to
express itself."[37]

All this was happening after just the first gold medal. Bolt's
primary event, the 200-meter run, and the 4x100-meter relay
were still to come.

Now the Two Hundred Meters

Michael Johnson, an American, had set the world record for the two hundred meters in the 1996 Olympics in Atlanta, with a time of 19.32 seconds. Johnson was convinced the mark would hold up. Bolt decided to take it easy during the preliminary heats, reinforcing that opinion. But when the finals came, lightning struck again.

There was no holding back this time. Bolt ran hard all the way, even dipping his chest to improve his time as he crossed the finish line. He easily outran the field with a new record time: 19.30 seconds, or 0.02 seconds faster than Johnson. Johnson was amazed: "Incredible. What an incredible start. Guys of 6-5 should not be able to start like that. It's that long, massive stride. He's eating up so much more track than the others. He came in focused, knowing he would likely win the gold and now he's got it."[38]

Bolt defeated Churandy Marina of Netherlands Antilles by four body lengths. Afterward, the Bird's Nest sound system played "Happy Birthday" as a salute to Bolt's twenty-second birthday, coming up at midnight. Bolt danced and swayed to the music, then pointed toward the scoreboard. He had become the first man since the revered Donald Quarrie to hold both the one-hundred-meter and two-hundred-meter world records simultaneously, and the first to set them by winning gold in both during the same Olympics.

Shared Glory

To finish his work in Beijing, Bolt ran the third leg of the 4x100 relays, with his good friend Powell at the anchor position. Halfway through, it was still an undecided race, with Nesta Carter and Michael Frater running the first two legs. Then Frater handed the baton to Bolt, and it was no longer undecided. The Jamaican team set a new Olympic record of 37.10 seconds.

Bolt and Powell had discussed this event a few nights before, when it became apparent that it would be Powell's only shot at gold. They did not just want to win, they wanted to break into the record book. And so they did.

(From left to right) Asafa Powell, Nesta Carter, Usain Bolt, and Michael Frater celebrate their record-breaking gold medal performance in the men's 4x100–meter relay at the Beijing Olympic Games.

For Bolt it was three golds and three world records—a performance like no one ever had witnessed before. In the space of just five days, the long-striding Jamaican "country boy," whose name was known only to avid track fans, had become one of the most closely watched athletes in the world.

In Kingston's Mandela Park, roads had been blocked off and giant video screens set up. After each of Bolt's Olympic victories proud Jamaicans took the party into the streets and danced until dawn.

Chapter 4

The Drug Issue

The questions started almost as soon as Usain Bolt crossed the hundred-meter finish line of the 2008 Olympics: Was he on drugs? And if he was not, how could he or anyone lower their time in the event as quickly as he did? "I'm still working with the fact that he dropped from 10-flat to 9.6 (seconds) in one year," said American gold-medal-winning sprinter Carl Lewis. "If you don't question that in a sport that has the reputation it has right now, you're a fool."[39]

Other commentators joined in the chorus of criticism, claiming they would bet a lot of money that Bolt was using drugs, because it seemed impossible to lower times so drastically in an event he had just taken up. Bolt, however, never had failed a drug test. He expressed indifference to Lewis's remarks. "When you run the 100 meters," he said, "that's what you get."[40]

Guilt by Association?

The reputation in track that Lewis alluded to was that many runners had been caught doping. Sprinters had come under a deep, dark cloud. Even while Lewis and Bolt were sniping at each other, two other members of the Jamaican relay team tested positive for a banned stimulant. Both had been coached at one time by Bolt's trainer, Glen Mills.

The cloud of suspicion began hovering over the track world well before the Olympics in Beijing, China. Some of the sport's most glittering names were stripped of their medals and even

Ben Johnson, second from left, gestures to Carl Lewis, far right, as he wins the 100 meter race at the Seoul, South Korea, 1988 Olympic Games. Johnson was later stripped of his medal for failing a drug test.

their freedom. Over the years, of the seven men who had run the hundred meters in 9.8 seconds or less, three had been busted for using performance-enhancing drugs: Justin Gatlin, Tim Montgomery and, most shockingly, the 1988 Olympic record-breaking gold medalist, Ben Johnson, who ran for Canada. Women's medalist and record holder Marion Jones did time in prison for lying to a grand jury when she denied using such drugs.

Mills defended Bolt. "We know questions are inevitable, given the revelations in the sport," said Mills. "But that doesn't trouble us for two reasons. One, there is a thing called conscience. Two, Usain doesn't even want to take Vitamin C. We know he is as clean as a whistle."[41]

Other Athletes Speak Up

The Jamaican-born Johnson continued to strongly deny that he ever took banned steroids, insisting that he was "set up" with steroid-spiked orange juice because of his intense rivalry with American sprinter Carl Lewis. Johnson says, "Whatever anyone says about me and steroids, I would never have done that, never have risked the damage that could do to your body."[42]

The steroids at issue are, specifically, anabolic steroids. They are growth hormones. They stimulate the body to create muscle-building proteins faster than is normal. Some athletes have found them to be a shortcut to power and speed; however, they can also lead to liver damage and other negative side effects. Beyond the physical enhancements steroids provide, of course, is the ethical issue of sporting fairness. Would allowing steroids mean a permanent advantage for drug-aided sports participants compared to the so-called natural athletes?

Young and Very Big

Back in the 1950s, the Detroit Lions professional football team had a lineman who weighed more than 300 pounds (136kg). Photographers from national publications visited the Lions' training camp just to snap pictures of Les Bingaman being weighed in on an agricultural feed scale. He was regarded as something of a freak.

Half a century later Bingaman would barely raise an eyebrow, because it has become common for even high school players to surpass that weight level—and not always by just eating and lifting weights. Some athletes also use steroids to bulk up.

Much of the concern about steroid usage has centered on the damage it does to young athletes unaware of its long-term effects on their bodies. All many of them know is that steroids give them a competitive edge on the field.

Perhaps the most damaging aftereffect involves the closing down of the body's growth centers, creating noticeably stockier and shorter athletes, like human fire hydrants, as they reach their late twenties.

The questions persist because of the inevitable pressures in the top levels of sports, where the attractions of money, fame, and athletic supremacy are so intoxicating and where losing even a little bit of ability is so feared. "Bullet" Bob Hayes, who once held the title of world's fastest man and was a star receiver for the Dallas Cowboys in the 1960s, was convicted of delivering narcotics to an undercover cop. "I'll tell you this," said Hayes, who died in 2002, "once you become fastest man, you can only go down."[43]

Wherever the truth may lie, the fact is that allegations of performance-enhancing drugs have tarnished the track world's glamour. Stephen Francis, who was Asafa Powell's coach, says of the controversy: "It doesn't mean he's [Bolt's] cheating; he's just using what he has. Usain ran 19.9 seconds in the 200 meters when he was a skinny kid of 17. Look at him now and 19.3 isn't that surprising."[44]

"We've been tested a lot," said Bolt at Beijing. "I was tested four times before I even started running here—urine, blood tests, so many I've lost track. I have no problem with that. We work hard, we're clean, and anytime they want to test us is fine."[45]

The Sports Connection

Baseball's steroid scandal attracted wider attention in the United States. But around the rest of the world the drug abuse reported in track was just as staggering. As it turned out, there was a connection: Balco Labs, based outside San Francisco, California, was the supplier of performance-enhancing drugs for both sports.

Balco's president, Victor Conte, had set out to create a marketing campaign for his new steroid product. He called it "the Clear" and it was undetectable in drug tests in 2001 when he introduced it. Teaming with record-breaking sprinter Montgomery, Conte hoped to sell it as a "natural" testosterone-boosting supplement for athletes.

Montgomery also took up weight training and a nutritional program under the guidance of his coach, Trevor Graham, and with Conte's supervision. But after Montgomery and others showed up at the Modesto Relays in California wearing T-shirts

Balco president Victor Conte poses with shelves of his nutritional supplements. He was accused by the U.S. Anti-Doping Agency of supplying athletes with undetectable designer steroids.

that read "Project World Record" it was too much even for Graham, who split with Conte and alerted investigators to the steroid use. The final result was exposure of the doping culture in sports, with alleged use also involving baseball superstars Barry Bonds and Roger Clemens.

Conte, whose first career was in music as a bass player, had become a self-taught expert on performance-enhancing substances. He had also become a cynic, coming to the conclusion that all the top runners were using something extra that was against the rules. He declared: "I had no idea how corrupt the Olympics were. . . . I learned there are two sets of rules: the ones in the book and the ones everybody plays by."[46]

The effect was apparent with Montgomery. He weighed just 148 pounds (67kg) when he joined Conte's group, and his nickname was "Tiny Tim." In one year he added 20 pounds (9kg) and clocked career bests in the sixty-meter and one-hundred-meter dashes, finishing second at the 2001 World Championships. He also earned six hundred thousand dollars for the season. He broke the one-hundred-meter record in 2002, a mark that later was taken away from him because of the steroid use. Montgomery also did prison time for heroin distribution. He said later that he was not forced to take steroids, but it was clear to him that to compete at the highest levels, steroids were necessary.

Ben Johnson had been at the highest level of all. In his 1988 gold medal sprint at the Seoul, South Korea, Olympics, in front of a crowd of seventy thousand, with hundreds of millions more people watching on television, Johnson exploded out of the starting blocks and thundered down the track, breaking his own world-record time and finishing at 9.79 seconds. Lewis, the 1984 quadruple gold medalist, was 0.13 seconds behind. But afterward, extensively thorough testing of Johnson's body fluids found an unmistakable presence of anabolic steroids.

Less than three days after his triumph, Johnson slunk away from Seoul in disgrace. The gold medal was transferred to Lewis. Johnson's adamant prerace denials of using any banned substance poisoned the atmosphere of world-class track competition.

Clean Is Tough to Prove

Since Johnson's disqualification in Seoul, every record-breaking run has been viewed with suspicion. So, of course Bolt's performances, which lowered world records so dramatically, stood out with warning flags. Of all the record holders since the 1980s, only Lewis had remained untainted. Even he came under suspicion, though, when a tiny amount of banned substance was detected in his system after a race. The suspicious substance was later ruled a cold remedy in an amount too small to matter.

With the ascendance of the latest star, the New York tabloids ran headlines calling him "A Bolt from the Blue." But he was not from the blue; he was from Jamaica, a place that runners who once held nine of the ten best times in the hundred meters called home. But this fact also raised suspicions, as a large number of Jamaican runners have failed their drug tests. Yet, there are as many explanations for this as there are Jamaican runners.

There was no solid evidence that Bolt himself was unclean, but a highly demoralizing part of the scandal was the virtual impossibility of the clean to prove their innocence. Every new record-breaking run could be construed as evidence that the hundred meters remained a dirty event, undermined by drugs. Going into Beijing, the event's reputation had never been so low. Nonetheless the duels among Bolt, Powell, and Gay since 2008 resulted in some of the most exciting competition the hundred meters had ever seen.

Immediately after the third of his gold-medal runs in Beijing, Bolt nonchalantly attributed his success to yams and chicken, especially nuggets. He declared that a perfect day for him would

At a press conference in Beijing, Bolt attributed his success to yams and chicken nuggets and not steroids. He passed every drug test given to him.

begin with some nuggets in bed, a little TV, and a nap followed by another round of nuggets.

Another overlooked aspect of the Jamaican team's sudden success was that most of its sprinters now trained in their own country, instead of going overseas through the collegiate system in the United States. The comforts of home—familiar food, settings, culture, team encouragement—seemed to help the Jamaicans thrive.

A Scientific View

The two sides of the steroid story are apparent in the experience of Jamaican sprinter Merlene Ottey. After a 1999 meet in Lucerne, Switzerland, Ottey tested positive for steroids. The International Association of Athletics Federations (IAAF) banned her from competing in the 2000 Olympics in Sydney, Australia. But she declared she had no knowledge of taking steroids, and she pressed an appeal. In the summer of 2000, the IAAF and the Jamaica Amateur Athletic Association cleared Ottey of all charges. Criticism then turned to the lab that had tested her the year before.

Gary Gaffney, who studied performance-enhancing drugs at the University of Iowa Medical School, says the standard drug tests of athletes are typically done at the wrong time: "It's during the off season that using anabolic steroids, along with intensive weight training, is most effective. That gives runners an explosive strength base for the competitive season. The Jamaicans claim they were tested extensively at the Olympics. But they didn't even have a national drug agency before that."[47]

Even so, Gaffney says part of the reason for the success of Jamaican sprinters might lie in the presence of a gene, among the twenty thousand or so appearing naturally in the human body, called Actinen A. About 70 percent of the top Jamaican runners have it in their muscle fibers, and it definitely stimulates muscle-fiber activity and running ability. Other studies identify a related gene, ACTN3, as the contributing performance gene.

Testing conducted at the University of Technology in Kingston, Jamaica, and at the MVP Track Club, home base for

Invisible Damage

Acommon abuse of performance-enhancing drugs is called stacking. It includes taking steroids in combination with other drugs. The belief is that this will enhance performance even more than steroids alone.

Some researchers are skeptical that steroids improve performance. But researchers are unanimous that the drugs will grow facial hair on women and give men a facial bloat.

Far more dangerous is the invisible harm steroids have on the body. Liver damage, blood-clotting disorders, and elevated cholesterol are common side effects of steroids. Psychological mood swings are also part of the program. They can run the gamut from depression to a sense of invincibility and include a fly-off-the-handle tendency that has become known as roid rage.

"The races in Beijing were amazing and I hope it's the turning point for track and field," says Jon Drummond, an assistant coach on the U.S. team. He contends it was grossly unfair to credit drugs for the new fastest-time records. "Technology is changing, the tracks are changing, the spikes [shoes] are getting lighter," Drummond says. "And look at them [the runners]. They're all over six feet. They're gentle giants, man."

Quoted in Christopher Clarey. "Bolt Shatters 100-Meter World Record. " *New York Times,* August 16, 2009, p. D1.

Olympic assistant coach Jon Drummond believes it is grossly unfair to credit drugs with faster times. He attributes the times to changing track-and-field technology and taller athletes.

Powell and other top sprinters, supports the genetic distinction. The gene has been traced to West Africa, where the ancestors of many Jamaicans used to live. The studies found Actinen A in 70 percent of the Jamaicans tested, compared with 30 percent in a control group of Australians.

Genes alone do not guarantee sprinting success, of course. Daniel MacArthur, one of the authors of a 2003 study reporting on the connections between the ACTN3 gene and sports competition, cautions that "super-elite athletes need to have the right ACTN3 combination, but they also have to have a whole host of other factors working in their favor. This one gene is just a minor ingredient in a large and complex recipe."[48]

Determining the exact cause of athletic prowess is tricky indeed. Another scientist who has studied ACTN3 is Dr. Stephen M. Roth, director of the functional genomics laboratory at the University of Maryland School of Public Health. According to Roth, at least two hundred different genes affect athletic performance, as do many other factors. As Roth says, "The idea that it will be one or two genes that are contributing to the [swimming champ] Michael Phelpses or Usain Bolts of the world I think is shortsighted because it's much more complex than that."[49]

Other academics say the history of slavery is what gives Jamaican athletes toughness. But Evelyn Higginbotham, professor of African American Studies at Harvard University, points out that other groups of people who also were enslaved have not produced world-class sprinters.

Diana Thorburn, a professor at the University of the West Indies, may be closer to the mark. She says that there are simply fewer options for people with world-class athletic potential in Jamaica, and that is why such a high proportion become runners, growing up in a sport that is relatively cheap to participate in. "If Usain Bolt had been born in Europe or North America he would now be earning far more money as a basketball player, with the odds of a much longer and more lucrative career,"[50] she points out.

A different sport might have been more lucrative as well for Powell, who was displaced by Bolt as the fastest man on the island (as well as in the world). Powell never won an individual

Jamaican sprinter Merlene Ottey was banned in the 2000 Olympic Games for testing positive for steroids. She appealed the decision and was reinstated.

Olympic or World Championship gold medal. Even though he held the world record twice, he never had the same kind of earning power as athletes in more lucrative sports.

By all accounts, Powell is not the kind of man who insists on being the center of attention or who demands to have more money than anyone else. He fits the image of the clean competitor.

Nevertheless, even with no evidence that either Powell or Bolt had ever violated a substance ban, their innocence remained under attack. Johnson continued to be a haunting presence. In an interview in late 2007, he declared, "I believe that everyone on the international level is using performance-enhancing drugs."[51] He offered no proof but blamed the alleged drug use on the high amounts of prize money dangled before the competitors.

Chapter 5

An Even Faster Year

At age twenty-two, Usain Bolt was officially the fastest man in the world and quite possibly the fastest in all of recorded history. He was also the youngest fastest man. No matter how gifted a young sprinter is, it usually takes years of honing techniques for a runner to reach the level of setting world records. A look at previous record holders in the hundred meters is illuminating. Setting aside the champions whose results were disallowed because of illegal drug supplements, the under-ten-seconds elite begins with Carl Lewis, who set the mark of 9.86 seconds at the 1991 World Championships in Tokyo, Japan. Lewis, from the United States, was thirty years old at the time.

Leroy Burrell, another American, cut the record by a hair in Switzerland in 1994, running it in 9.85 seconds at age twenty-seven. Two years later, Jamaican-born Donovan Bailey of Canada sliced another hair off, covering the hundred meters in 9.84 seconds in the Olympics in Atlanta, Georgia. Bailey was twenty-eight.

A trend toward somewhat younger champions followed. The next two men to establish new world records for the one hundred meters were each just under twenty-five years old. American Maurice Greene ran a 9.79 in Athens, Greece, in 1999, and then the Jamaican Asafa Powell lowered the mark to 9.74 seconds during a meet in Italy.

Then came Bolt, younger than all the rest and at the same time a towering figure in world sport. After his dazzling display in the 2008 Olympics—the most-watched footraces ever—he kept right on competing in 2009. In the second half of the year, the results were even more dazzling.

American Maurice Green became the first runner under age twenty-five to hold the record for the one hundred meters when he clocked in at 9.79 in Athens in 1999. Bolt would be the youngest record holder ever.

Wildly Popular in Jamaica

The dynamic Bolt had become a heroic and hugely popular figure in his native land. The government assigned two bodyguards to shadow him on travel throughout Jamaica. The bodyguards had very little protecting to do—everyone seemed to love Bolt—but were needed sometimes to ensure the young star simply had some breathing room in his home country. He asked friends to do errands for him, because if he went to a store, for instance, he would be stopped in the streets by cheering mobs. Autograph requests filled his mailbox. His athletic achievements combined with his upbeat personality made him a huge favorite at late-night parties and clubs, and he clearly enjoyed the nightlife.

"I explain to people that I'm still young," he said. "I'm going to go out and enjoy myself. If that's going to be a problem, that's their problem."[52] Yet Bolt knew that dancing and partying were not sufficient training routines to stay atop the world of championship sprinting. As he said later that year at the World Championships, "When it comes to competition, I'm always ready."[53]

During 2009, Bolt started competing for a record in an event in which he had yet to achieve supremacy: the four hundred meters. Then a setback occurred. While driving his new BMW—driving barefoot, as usual—he slid the car off a Jamaican back road. He left the scene with a smile, saying everything was going to be fine. His only injury was from stepping on some thorns afterward. He had to have surgery to remove the thorns and missed a meet the following weekend. Soon, though, a *London Daily Mirror* headline declared: "Usain Bolt reveals how horror car crash made him change his life." Bolt was quoted as saying of the accident, "It has changed my outlook on life a little bit. You chew it all over and see where you have gone wrong."[54]

Recovering after the mishap, Bolt decided to put off his goal of longer-distance record breaking and set out instead to win a

Down Home

Even after Usain Bolt gained worldwide acclaim and millions in income, his father, Wellesley, continued operating his simple grocery shop in the interior of Jamaica where his now-famous son grew up.

"I told him, 'Yo, Dad, stop working,'" the younger Bolt says. "'I can take care of you guys.' He's like, 'Nah.' He wants something to do. He's a guy who likes to be independent."

Wellesley Bolt also worked in coffee-bean fields when his children were young, The family home had no running water. Bolt made young Usain carry full buckets for long distances. Today, Usain Bolt's broad shoulders and strong back bear witness to the power of weight training with water.

Quoted in Sean Gregory. "Runners-Up for Person of the Year." *Time*, December 16, 2009.

150-meter street race in the Manchester, England, City Games. The race was a unique event that had runners competing at various distances on England's city streets. Bolt ran the 150-meter in 14.35 seconds, the fastest time ever recorded in that event.

Bolt also competed in the European Golden League season in 2009. The Golden League was a series of one-day track-and-field meets in various European cities. The 2009 season was its twelfth, and it turned out to be its last. The league's demise was not because of failure. On the contrary, its popularity was such that, for 2010, the league was succeeded by plans for a bigger tour, with fourteen separate meets around the globe, known as the Diamond League.

Bolt, no stranger to gold—at least in medals—was drawn to Golden League participation not only to stay sharp against the world's best but by the promise of extra money. The director of the league's meet in Paris, France, Laurent Boquillet, acknowledged, "I decided to spend my budget on him" rather than "distribute it to some other athletes. I thought it was really important. I have to fill a stadium and right now, unfortunately, only Bolt can do that. So that was a priority."[55]

Bolt came through again in the Paris meet. On July 17, despite rain, a slight headwind, and a poor start, he won the hundred meters in a world-class time of 9.83 seconds.

Bolt's team had concluded it was best for him to stick with the one-hundred- and two-hundred-meter events in 2009 and put off serious consideration of the four hundred. Bolt won at the shorter distances in races in his home capital, Kingston, Jamaica, thus qualifying for the World Championships that August, a competition to be held in Berlin, Germany.

Taking on the World

The coming world meet attracted far more attention than usual, chiefly for two reasons. First of all, the glorious aura of Bolt's Olympic triumphs was still shining bright. Just as important was the history of the site. The events were to take place at the same stadium where victories by the African American runner Jesse

Bolt promotes the Great Manchester 150 race in Great Britain. Bolt ran the 150 meters street race in 14.35 seconds, the fastest time ever recorded in the event.

Owens had enraged Adolf Hitler and other white-supremacist Nazi leaders in the 1936 Olympics.

The sprint competition looked formidable, headed by previous world champion and record holder Tyson Gay, now twenty-six, of the United States. A little over a month earlier, on July 10, in a Golden League meet in Rome, Italy, that Bolt had skipped, Gay equaled his own U.S. record in the hundred meters with a time of 9.77 seconds. Gay edged Bolt's countryman Powell by 0.11 seconds.

"I feel I'm improving," Gay said. "I give myself a 100 percent chance to win"[56] in the World Championships.

In Berlin, in the one-hundred-meter preliminaries to the championship dash, Bolt breezed through a qualifying heat at 9.89 seconds—an outstanding time for many top-ranked competitors but done with ease by Bolt. Then came the tension-building night of August 16, the night of the sprint to establish who was now the fastest of them all. Would Bolt prove himself more enduring than a few Olympic flashes of glory?

A Straight-Line Showdown

This was the first time Bolt and Gay had squared off in 2009. Bolt displayed his signature archer lightning-bolt pose. Every man in the race had previously run the hundred in less than ten seconds. Bolt and Gay were in adjacent lanes.

The starting signal sounded and the competitors surged forward. Initially the runners were all about even—eyes forward in concentration, arms pumping, legs flashing. Then, with an explosive effort, Gay covered the distance in 9.71 seconds, his best competitive time ever and just 0.02 seconds slower than Bolt's record-setting Olympic time.

But another man got there first. Striding powerfully near the finish line, Bolt looked to his right as if to say "Gay, where are you?" The crowd erupted in appreciation as the clock showed Bolt had run the hundred meters in a new world record time of 9.58 seconds. Since electronic timing of races began, never had there been such a large margin of victory over a previous world record in the hundred. Bolt had covered the distance in forty-

At the 2009 IAAF World Championships, Tyson Gay, middle, ran a personal best time of 9.71 but still lost to Bolt who set a new world record of 9.58 seconds.

one strides, one sportswriter calculated, while the shorter Gay had taken forty-four.

Better than Great

How did Bolt surpass his already amazing Olympic record? Since the Beijing, China, competition, Bolt claimed to have improved his starting-block reaction time. In addition, it appeared he was getting his large muscles into full motion sooner in the race.

Was it possible Bolt could go any faster? "You never know," he said at the time. "I'll just keep on working."[57] With the perspective of a man focused far beyond one spectacular burst down the track, Bolt recognized the difficulty of staying at the top: "I think

I have to keep doing this year after year, and it's going to take a lot of hard work, because these guys are going to be coming next season and the season after that."[58]

Gay declined to blame a groin injury for his failure to match Bolt. "I showed a lot of heart," Gay said. "I put it together the best I could."[59] He did decide, though, to pull out of running the two hundred meters.

Unprecedented

The two-hundred-meter World Championships final came four days after the hundred. The starting blocks were on a curved portion of the track, so rather than line up side by side as in the hundred, the runners began in a staggered formation so that each, by staying in his lane, would run the same distance to the finish. Bolt was in one of the middle lanes.

Within an instant after the starting signal, Bolt was clearly moving ahead. His advantage grew as the men sprinted out of the curve and into the straight portion of the track. There was Bolt in the lead while everyone else appeared to be in some other race. So clearly bigger and faster, Bolt was a Ferrari compared with the compact Toyotas of the trailing group of world-class sprinters.

At the end Bolt had smashed another record. He finished in 19.19 seconds, beating his own mark by more than a tenth of a second. His was the biggest margin of victory in the two hundred meters in World Championship history. The second-place finisher, Alonso Edward of Panama, trailed by 7 meters (23 feet). Another of the also-rans, former Olympic champ Shawn Crawford, says: "I felt like I was in a video game; that guy was moving—fast."[60]

Later that year, reflecting on the stupendous races in Berlin, Bolt said, "I wasn't all that surprised about the 100. I knew it was going to be a fast race. But the 200 one, I was like, 'Whoa!' That caught me off guard."[61]

Adulation Pours Out

Before the medal ceremony for the two hundred meters, Bolt joyfully went over to the spectators and began signing autographs.

Highlights of the Records

Usain Bolt ended 2009 as the holder of three world and three Olympic records. In the 100 meters and 200 meters, he had both the fastest times ever run in the World Championships as well as the second fastest in the Olympics. In addition, the Olympics-winning Jamaican 400-meter relay team, of which Bolt was one of four members, had both the fastest and second-fastest times ever.

Bolt also racked up an extraordinary achievement when he competed in a 150-meter race in Britain in 2009. The 150 is not often run in world competition, so Bolt's record-setting time in that race was less of a distinction, but the amazing part was that he ran the last hundred meters of the race that day in 8.70 seconds—the fastest time ever recorded for a human being for that distance.

Standing on the victory podium became a regular occurrence for Bolt in 2009, as he held three new world and three Olympic records.

As a delighted crowd roared its approval, fans and even event volunteers took off their shirts and handed them to Bolt for his signature.

The four-hundred-meter relay competition was an anticlimax. Bolt and his fellow Jamaicans won the event in World Championship record time, but they were not quite as fast as they had been in the 2008 Olympics.

As the World Championships came to a close, the mayor of Berlin was far more gracious toward the dark-skinned world's fastest man than Hitler had been toward Owens. In a presentation ceremony, Klaus Wowereit gave Bolt a section of the Berlin Wall, which had long divided the German capital and East and West Germany during the Cold War and was taken down in 1987 when the country was reunited. Wowereit declared that Bolt had shown "one can tear down walls that had been considered as insurmountable."[62]

A Happy Pair of Runners

Bolt continued running in Europe as the year went on. In a Golden League meet in Zurich, Switzerland, on August 28, he and friendly rival Powell thrilled the crowd watching the one-hundred-meter final. At the seventy-meter mark, the hard-running Powell had the lead. But Bolt surged past to take the victory with a time of 9.81 seconds, beating his fellow Jamaican by 0.07 seconds.

The Golden League season concluded in Brussels, Belgium, on September 4. Despite a damp evening, a sell-out crowd of forty-seven thousand people showed up for a top-ranked set of competitions in various track-and-field events for women and men. This time Bolt ran in the two hundred meters and sped to victory in 19.57 seconds. Powell took on Gay in the hundred meters and won with a time of 9.90 seconds.

Both Jamaicans were lauded on their return to their country. Combined, they had now achieved nine of the ten fastest times ever certified in the hundred meters. What a tremendous year 2009 had been, especially for Bolt. He received his country's

Bolt makes his acceptance speech after being awarded the 2009 IAAF Athlete of the Year award.

equivalent of knighthood, the Order of Jamaica. The national tourism agency recruited him to be filmed in commercials promoting the country. The parties resumed, including fund-raisers attended by high rollers to benefit poorer Jamaicans.

International honors rolled in as well. On November 22, 2009, Bolt was named male winner of the IAAF World Athlete of the Year award. His joyous record-smashing victories had elevated track's image globally, and he had become an athletic hero for all the world to admire.

Time to Take a Break

Along with the glory came advice. Four-time Olympic gold medalist Michael Johnson wrote a *Newsweek* magazine piece that read, "It might be time for Bolt to slow down. Physically, there is no doubt he can continue to compete, and there is no telling how fast he might go one day. But mentally, it is a different story. The most difficult thing for a young, accomplished athlete to do is to figure out how to stay motivated."[63]

After all, Johnson reasoned, Bolt had accomplished in just two years what other world champions take a decade to do—the decade of their prime performance ability. The coming year, 2010, would not include either an Olympic or a World Championship event. It would be a fine time to relax.

Johnson offered one more reason for Bolt to limit his running to just a few competitions: lack of suspense. In any race Bolt enters, Johnson wrote, "we already know who is going to win."[64]

Chapter 6

2010 and Beyond

A t the pinnacle of his sport, as the holder of world records and Olympic gold medals, Usain Bolt reflected in an interview: "When you get the gold, what is there to do for you? What is next? You got to do something that is impossible to reach. I set myself a standard. I want to be a legend. So that is the biggest goal. If I stay on top and win all these awards, I'm sure to be a legend. I want to be a track-and-field legend. That's what I work for."[65]

Establishing himself as the greatest sprinter in history would take time. The year 2010 provided few opportunities. The next Olympic track events, to be held in London, were not scheduled until 2012. The next World Championships, conducted every other year by the International Association of Athletics Federations (IAAF), were not planned until 2011. The year 2010 offered time for planning, training, and deciding in what ways Bolt would build his legend.

He Could Go Longer

One possibility was conquering the four hundred meters. No one had ever dominated all three distances at the same time. Should Bolt resume the longer-distance training he had begun in 2009? Early each season now, Bolt ran the four hundred as part of his routine for building his stamina.

Among those who thought he should make the four hundred meters a priority was Michael Johnson, the former four-hundred-meter world champion. Johnson declared: "Every now and again, along comes an athlete for the times and I believe Usain Bolt is

Bolt competes for the first time in the four-hundred-meter race at the Camperdown Classic in Jamaica. He won with a time of 45.86 seconds.

that athlete. It happened to me in 1996. It happened with Carl Lewis in 1984 and Jesse Owens in 1936 . . . and now it is happening for Usain Bolt."[66]

In early 2010, while filming a documentary for the BBC, Johnson visited Bolt in Jamaica. Johnson reported: "He understands . . . that it will take a lot more work training for the 400 than for the 100 and 200."[67]

Bolt did compete in the four hundred in a Kingston, Jamaica, event. On February 13, 2010, he won handily with a time of 45.86 seconds, setting a record for the Camperdown Classic meet while looking relaxed at the finish. It was the fifth-fastest time recorded by Bolt for four hundred meters.

The Jamaican Way

Whatever the distance, Bolt preferred to do the training in his home country. He knew the importance of that decision to his fellow Jamaicans, who used to see the top athletes leave for the supposedly superior facilities and coaching available in Britain, which long ago had colonized Jamaica, or in Canada or the

The Money

Compared with baseball, football, and basketball, track has not been a big-money sport. Runners are known for their dedication rather than their wealth. The number of significant track events per year is relatively small, and stadium and broadcast revenues are tiny by the standards of major U.S. sports.

Just a few track stars have seen riches, and almost all of them have been those who run the shortest distance, the one hundred meters. Ben Johnson, the Jamaican-born Canadian, was making $480,000 per month from endorsements around the time of the 1988 Seoul Olympics. By one estimate, Johnson's disqualification for using illegal substances cost him as much as $100 million over the next ten years.

Usain Bolt's London-based agent, Ricky Simms, says Bolt could expect to receive $10 million a year in prize money, appearance fees, and endorsement income.

United States. Now Bolt, as well as Asafa Powell, displayed the success and expertise of their nation's methods.

Typically, world-class sprint training uses synthetic surfaces. The Jamaicans do some running on those but mostly they train on grass. This can be an advantage. Sprinting on a soft and uneven surface means muscles have to work harder and tendons stretch more. Thus the runners can become stronger.

The Jamaicans also do uphill sprints year-round, attempting to accelerate to top speed despite the slope. After that, running on flat ground feels like a breeze.

In addition, the Jamaicans' training routine includes going all out for distances up to six times as far as they would run in competition. Again, running a regular race can become easier than the training, because the runners have already built up their stamina, strengthened their flexibility, and maximized their bodies' ability to produce energy by the time they take to the track.

Mr. Casual

Even so, Bolt sustained a casual image about his race preparations. Even at the Olympics, where the massive public attention and crucial stakes bring high tension to many athletes, Bolt appeared totally relaxed. Asked later what he did in Beijing during the day before his hundred-meters victory, Bolt said: "Ah, I never had breakfast. Woke up at 11 a.m. Sat around. Watched TV. Had lunch—some nuggets. Then went back to my room. Slept three hours. Got some more nuggets. Came down to the track."[68]

Bolt's mother, Jennifer, says her son has a genuinely playful nature: "Usain likes to clown around. That's how he plays with me and with his girlfriend. It's not unusual to find him wrestling with his dad. He's having fun."[69]

The girlfriend Jennifer Bolt refers to is Mizicann Evans, known as Mitzy. The couple had known each other since childhood and by 2010 had been a romantic pair for five years. Evans says success did not change Bolt. She says he was "always happy, always wanting to make everybody around him laugh."[70]

Mizicann Evans poses with Bolt in Beijing. They have been friends since childhood and were romantically involved for several years.

Even in 2010 the question kept surfacing: Was staying relaxed the key secret to Bolt's ability to achieve world records, or could he go even faster if he trained harder? Sometimes it appeared he was more devoted to his Xbox than to the track. Noting that, one writer declared: "What would happen if the greatest athlete alive put as much effort into his training as he does his video games?"[71]

Yet to Reach His Limit

In March 2010 Bolt was living in his hillside condo overlooking the National Stadium in Kingston, pondering the possibilities —and tasting the nightlife from time to time, hitting such clubs as the Quad, his longtime favorite, and Fiction. Of the latter, he says, "It's sort of middle-class but I like going there. And of course I know all the DJs. When they come to the end of the night they let me mess around [as a DJ] sometimes. But I'm only in practice as a DJ."[72]

As a runner, Bolt said he would stay in top shape, yet not train hard enough to set any world records in 2010: "Of course, if I need to run as fast as 9.5 to stay unbeaten I have to do it. But if I just have to run 9.9 to win every race, then that's what I want— because next year is different. I have to get back to 9.5 next year."[73] Bolt was referring to the 2011 World Championships. That time would surpass Bolt's world mark of 9.58 seconds.

The fastest man on earth then declared he had never yet gone all-out in the one hundred meters. "The best is still to come," Bolt said. "I've never run just straight and focused on getting to the finish line. I'm always looking over at the other guys to see where they are. So one day, if I can stay focused and run really fast right through, then I could do it."[74]

Now, that was a challenge for his opponents. Could anyone push Bolt to the maximum? Actually, Bolt says, his next-door neighbor could, referring to Powell, whose condo adjoins Bolt's on the Kingston hillside. Powell, his relay teammate and favorite rival, is also capable of a 9.5-second hundred, Bolt says.

Back to Running

In April Bolt led a Jamaican team to the Penn Relays, the oldest and most celebrated annual track meet in the United States. Bolt had not run in the United States since before setting his 2009 World Championship records in Berlin. In Philadelphia a record crowd of more than fifty-four thousand came out on the final day of the meet, largely to see Bolt run his quarter of the

To relax, Bolt likes the nightlife and practicing being a DJ at clubs.

Ultimate Speed

Usain Bolt's stunning runs have prompted scientists to reexamine the question of just how fast a human being can run. He has hit nearly 28 miles per hour (45km per hour). Is there a limit?

The key to winning sprints is not moving your legs faster than the other runners but having your feet hit the ground with greater force and quickness. This is done through muscle contraction, which is still something of a mystery. Peter Weyand, an expert in applied physiology and biomechanics, says, "We still have an incomplete understanding of the process of force production within the body, and how the body's internal forces eventually translate into motion."

Weyand writes that even faster speeds might be achieved by biological interventions that speed up muscle contraction, or through dietary or training techniques, or improvements in shoes or even prosthetic devices.

Peter Weyand. "Usain Bolt and the Limits of Human Speed." *Christian Science Monitor,* September 4, 2009, p. 9.

four-hundred-meter relay. Wild cheering erupted at the mere sight of Bolt coming out to the infield to loosen up for his run.

He did not disappoint. Taking off from what had become known as the stadium's "whoop corner"—the curve where a heavily Jamaican crowd roared its approval—Bolt covered the distance in a blazing 8.79 seconds and helped his team break the Penn Relays record for the event.

Darvis Patton, a member of the defeated U.S. team, summed up his situation with a comparison to the world of basketball. "I'm competing in the era of Jordan," he said. "It's awesome."[75]

Bolt, in Jamaica's green and yellow colors, waved to and blew kisses to the crowd, which responded with great affection. Later Bolt recalled warmly that he had competed in the Penn Relays for four straight years while a Jamaican high school student and that being there this time was like appearing before a home crowd. "It was all fun,"[76] he beamed.

The following month, Bolt was on the other side of the globe, competing in two Diamond League track meets. In South Korea, he chose to run the hundred meters, and he won. In China, the choice was the two hundred, where he dominated. Then a slight Achilles tendon injury put Bolt on the sidelines for six weeks. That gave him the opportunity to follow the National Basketball Association (NBA) playoffs in the United States more closely. A fan of Boston Celtics forward Kevin Garnett, Bolt attended the fifth game of the finals in Boston, Massachusetts, which the Celtics won before the Los Angeles Lakers closed them out in games six and seven in Los Angeles, California.

Powell seized the spotlight created by Bolt's absence from the track. In the Diamond League meet in Oslo, Norway, on June 4, Powell sped through the hundred meters in a personal best 9.72 seconds, setting up a showdown in Britain with the American contender, Tyson Gay.

Rivalries Resume

On July 8, Bolt returned to action successfully in a Diamond League meet in Lausanne, Switzerland. Taking his doctor's advice and choosing the hundred meters for this day's test, Bolt stayed undefeated for the year with a 9.82 time.

Two days later in Gateshead, England, Powell and Gay lined up side by side for a renewal of their intense rivalry in the one hundred. As they lifted their heads at the starting blocks, the wind blew against them from the finish line. The starting signal sounded, and in 9.94 seconds Gay had prevailed by 0.02 seconds, against the wind.

Bolt decided to compete next in a Diamond League meet in Paris, France on July 16, again choosing the hundred meters. Powell joined the field as well. It was the first time the two star Jamaicans had squared off in 2010. Powell was the last man to have beaten Bolt in the hundred, two years previously in Stockholm, Sweden.

The day before the race—a day many athletes usually spend intensely focusing on preparations—Bolt was part of a Jamaican street party. Amid the crowd of a couple thousand, Bolt the DJ spun Bob Marley tunes.

Race day brought mild weather; conditions were excellent, but Bolt started poorly. Halfway through the race, Powell led. Then Bolt surged to win in 9.84 seconds, with Powell second at 9.91. Another Jamaican, Yohan Blake, was third at 9.95. It was the fourteenth consecutive victory for Bolt in a one-hundred-meter final.

"It wasn't the best race I've ever had in my life," Bolt acknowledged. "My first part was awful. . . . It's all about determination."[77] Asked about his competition, including the possibility that runners other than Powell and Gay could pose any challenge, Bolt said:

> You can never know who is going to show up on the day. I focus on everybody in the race and I take them all seriously, whether it's Asafa or Tyson or everybody else. These guys are good. I train with them all the time so I know how good. Over time, with work and focus, they're only going to get better. I know these guys are coming up and so I keep my eyes on them.[78]

It was now two years since Bolt had lost a hundred-meter race. Was the pressure of trying to stay undefeated too much? The racing scene shifted to Stockholm for the Diamond League meet on August 6, where the prize for the hundred was a ten-thousand-dollar diamond. Powell, with a back injury, decided to skip this event, but Gay was there.

The gun sounded. As often happened, Bolt trailed early, but pulled closer to the lead. Halfway through the dash he was a fraction behind Gay. Then, to the astonishment of many in the crowd, Gay pulled away and won with a time of 9.84 seconds—defeating Bolt for the first time. Bolt was second at 9.97 seconds, which, given his earlier achievements, seemed almost pokey.

That Gay did so well was, in itself, not surprising. A superb runner, he would have been recognized as the world's top

At the IAAF meet in Stockholm, American Tyson Gay, center, defeated Bolt for the first time. Bolt praised Gay and said, "I am not unbeatable."

sprinter in most other eras. It was a measure of Bolt's current dominance that this Stockholm result shocked many fans.

Bolt retained his perspective: "Just one of those days. I told you I'm not unbeatable. I did not train as hard as in past years, so I can't complain. And it was Tyson Gay. My congratulations to him. I'm not in my best shape and he is in great shape. I simply wasn't ready for that clash."[79]

Heavily Friended

Back in Jamaica, Bolt marked a different kind of milestone. As he put it: "I recently reached 2 million fans on my Facebook which was good—WOW!"[80] Typically, Bolt's Facebook postings are upbeat, polite, appreciative of his fans and highly supportive of other Jamaican athletes. With a generous spirit, he pays particular attention to singling out the triumphs and worthy efforts of other runners from his nation. A typical Bolt Facebook posting reads: "What a great day for me—My Racers Track Club teammates and fellow Jamaicans, Jermaine Gonzales, just ran 44.40 seconds in the 400 metres in Monaco. It is a National Record and a world leading time. Ricardo Chambers also ran his personal best in the same race 44:54. Racers to the worl'!!!"[81]

Bolt continues to show the same spirit in trying to use his fame and money to open doors for many young women and men in Jamaica, whether they are athletes or not. Proud of his heritage, Bolt expresses an ideal of succeeding while staying based in the island nation.

No matter how amiable he is, Bolt's friendly nature does not prevent recognition of the competitive emotions of his sport. In a BBC radio interview September 1, 2010, he offered this characterization of his chief U.S. rival: "I think Tyson sits at home and cusses me. He just really gets upset because every time he runs fast, I run faster. . . . So deep down I think he probably just hates my guts."[82]

Big Money, Less Money

Bolt could have made much more money if he had moved to the United States or Britain. In general, top athletes receive the greatest share of their wealth not from prize money in their events but from endorsements. The *Forbes* magazine 2009 list of athletes making the most money was topped by professional golfer Tiger Woods at $110 million. Michael Jordan is not even playing basketball anymore, but made $45 million, as did Los

Angeles Lakers star Kobe Bryant. Englishman David Beckham, playing soccer in Los Angeles and Madrid, Spain, pulled in $42 million.

Lewis Hamilton, an Afro-British athlete the same age as Bolt who, like Bolt, won a world championship while exceptionally young, made $32 million. Hamilton, a Formula 1 race car driver, was almost instantly an endorsement favorite.

Combining the expectations for prize money, appearance fees, and endorsements, Bolt's agent had set a comparatively modest income goal of $10 million a year. That is, it was a modest sum compared to the earnings of other sports superstars but reportedly a higher amount than any track competitor had ever pulled in.

Bolt's major deals are with Gatorade, which signs many athletes; the cell phone company Digicel Group; and Puma, the shoe-and-clothing line. Bolt's flashing feet, in their golden-yam-colored Pumas, were a hit among track fans, but financially nowhere near the Nike value of even a tarnished Tiger Woods, whose sport carries a more lasting appeal to more affluent consumers.

Then, in late August, Puma announced it had negotiated a new three-year contract with Bolt, worth more than any track-star pact in history. The company cited his winning personality as well as physical ability. Exact figures were not disclosed, but Puma indicated the endorsements-and-designs deal was worth about $8 million a year to Bolt. The contract did not boost him to the highest ranks but was a clear sign that he towered commercially as well as physically in the world of track.

A Good Life Indeed

Whatever his earning potential would turn out to be, Bolt was certainly well off and, by all accounts, happy in 2010. He and Puma launched a line of footwear and apparel designed by Bolt. The predominant colors are Bolt's favorites—purple, black, and green. Items range from on-the-track wear such as speed shorts with a friction-reducing inner brief to a lightweight hooded

Bolt is mobbed by Swedish fans at the launch of his self-designed Puma Bolt Collection of shoes and sportswear in Stockholm in August 2010.

sweat jacket with lightning-stripe stitching and a hidden compartment for an MP3 player.

There appears to be a unity to Bolt's life. The clothes, the parties, the friendships, the athletic competition, and the personal sense of self are all rooted in a joyfully Jamaican way of living. Even the hardest work, that being the training necessary to stay atop the running world, fits into the pattern. Bolt expresses this attitude while talking with a reporter about his outwardly disciplinarian coach, Glen Mills: "For you guys the coach is hard. He doesn't like the media. But we laugh every day. He gives us a program and I try to get out of it, and so we're always laughing. He's not like a guy who hits down with the hammer all the time. If you know what you need to do, it's all fun with him."[83]

Another apparent reason for sparing the hammer in Bolt's situation is his history with injuries and the vulnerability caused by his height. As the researchers had declared, he is simply too tall to keep on succeeding. Mills was well aware of all this from the beginning of their relationship: "When I got him, he was injured. Also, his coordination and all those things were off. And his scoliosis was affecting his hamstring. So we had to do some work."[84]

But an essential part of the work, under Mills's direction, is to not work constantly. Instead, the training concentrates on flexibility and core strength, rather than constant intensity.

Bolt achieves balance as well in how he deals with both fame and criticism. Instead of trying to please everyone's conflicting demands and perceptions, he notes, "I figured it out, and I was like, OK . . . I've got to put me first. And then I just started enjoying it."[85]

Looking to 2012

Bolt was especially happy that the next Olympics would be in London. If the 2012 games could not be in Jamaica, London might be the next best place, for the city has a large Jamaican population. "Oh, man, I'm so excited," Bolt says, adding:

> I've been telling people it's going to be nerve-racking if you're not mentally prepared. If you're not ready for that, then don't go. Jamaicans are loud—very loud. They're not like other crowds who just sit around. And they don't just cheer after the race. They cheer before the race and then they go crazy. So that's why I'm looking forward to London.[86]

Because Bolt's career zoomed upward so early in his life, he will be heading into his third Olympic Games while still only twenty-six. Looking onward, victories in a fourth Olympics at age thirty seem like a reasonable expectation. Carl Lewis was thirty when he set what was then the world record in the hundred-meter dash.

For the world's fastest man, now, the path to his cherished goal of legendary status is not only clear but clearly possible. Usain Bolt has the chance to prove himself the best of all time.

Introduction: The Happy Sprinter

1. Quoted in Leon Mann. "What Makes Usain Bolt Tick?" *BBC Sport,* May 14, 2009. http://news.bbc.co.uk/go/pr/fr/-/sport2/hi/athletics/8049584.stm.
2. Quoted in "Bolt Joins List of Youth Olympic Ambassadors." *Emirates 24/7,* July 6, 2010. www.emirates247.com/sports/other/.
3. Quoted in "Bolt Joins List of Youth Olympic Ambassadors."

Chapter 1: A Surprising Beginning

4. Quoted in Anna Kessel. "Usain Bolt's Rise from Rags to Rapid Riches." *Observer* (London), August 9, 2009, p. 12.
5. Quoted in Anna Kessel. "Olympics: Jamaican Speed Freak." *Observer* (London), August 24, 2008, p. 8.
6. Quoted in Mann. "What Makes Usain Bolt Tick?"
7. Quoted in Mann. "What Makes Usain Bolt Tick?"
8. Quoted in Kessel. "Olympics: Jamaican Speed Freak."
9. Quoted in Kessel. "Olympics: Jamaican Speed Freak."
10. Owen Slot. "Usain Bolt and the Making of an Olympic Champion." *Times* (London), September 11, 2008. www.timesonline.co.uk/tol/sport/more_sport/athletics/article4727520.ece.
11. Quoted in Slot. "Usain Bolt and the Making of an Olympic Champion."
12. Quoted in Kessel. "Usain Bolt's Rise from Rags to Rapid Riches."
13. Quoted in Kessel. "Olympics: Jamaican Speed Freak."
14. Quoted in Kessel. "Usain Bolt's Rise from Rags to Rapid Riches."
15. Quoted in Kessel. "Olympics: Jamaican Speed Freak."

Chapter 2: The Rivals

16. Quoted in Edward McClelland. "Taking Sprinting to New Heights." *Slate,* August 17, 2008. www.slate.com/id/2197679.

17. Quoted in Tom Fordyce. "I Can Win Olympic Gold—Powell." *BBC Sport*, July 24, 2008. http://news.bbc.co.uk/sport2/hi/olympics/athletics/7523910.stm.

Chapter 3: Olympic Showdown

18. Quoted in Tom Fordyce. "I Can Win Olympic Gold—Powell."
19. Quoted in Gary Smith. "Friends for Life: Powell Says He Won't Trash Talk Bolt." World-Track.org, July 23, 2009. www.world-track.org/2009/07/friends-for-life-powell-says/.
20. Quoted in Mike Fish. "Lost Legacy of the World's Fastest Man." ESPN.com, August 13, 2009. http://sports.espn.go.com/oly/trackandfield/columns/story?columnist=fish_mike&id=4395056.
21. Quoted in *The Official Website of Tyson Gay*. "Tyson's Biography." www.tysongay.net/bio.php.
22. Quoted in Mark Maloney. "Catch Him if You Can: Lexingtonian Is Split Second Away from Being World's Fastest Human." *Lexington (KY) Herald-Leader*, March 4, 2007, p. A1.
23. Quoted in Tim Layden. "The Phenom." *Sports Illustrated*, August 16, 2008. http://sportsillustrated.cnn.com/vault/article/magazine/MAG1142292/index.htm.
24. Quoted in Smith. "Friends for Life—Powell Says He Won't Trash Talk Bolt."
25. Tim Layden. "Bolt's Performance Freezes Time." *Sports Illustrated,* August 16, 2008, http://sportsillustrated.cnn.com/2008/olympics/2008/writers/tim_layden/08/16/mens.100/.
26. Quoted in Kessell. "Olympics: Jamaican Speed Freak."
27. Quoted in Brendan Gallagher. "Beijing Olympics: Usain Bolt Set to Run in Both the 100 and 200 Metres." *Daily Telegraph* (London), August 5, 2008. www.telegraph.co.uk/sport/other sports/olympics/2506738/2008-Beijing-Olympics-Usain-Bolt-set-to-run-in-both-the-100-and-200-metres-Olympic.html.
28. Quoted in Gallagher. "Beijing Olympics: Usain Bolt Set to Run in Both the 100 and 200 Metres."

29. Quoted in Gallagher. "Beijing Olympics: Usain Bolt Set to Run in Both the 100 and 200 Metres."

30. Quoted in Gallagher. "Beijing Olympics: Usain Bolt Set to Run in Both the 100 and 200 Metres."

31. Quoted in Gallagher. "Beijing Olympics: Usain Bolt Set to Run in Both the 100 and 200 Metres."

32. Quoted in Tristan. "Sports Hero: Usain Bolt," *The My Hero Project*. www.myhero.com/go/hero.asp?hero=U_bolt_LC_ guthriePS_CA_09_ul.

33. Quoted in Fish. "Lost Legacy of the World's Fastest Man."

34. Quoted in Fish. "Lost Legacy of the World's Fastest Man."

35. Quoted in Layden. "Bolt's Performance Freezes Time."

36. Quoted in Kessel. "Olympics: Jamaican Speed Freak."

37. Quoted in The Canadian Press. "IAAF Sides with Jamaican Sprinter Bolt on Rogge Comment." *TSN*, August 23, 2008.

38. Quoted in Associated Press. "Jamaica's Usain Bolt Breaks World Record in 200-Meter Dash." August 20, 2008. www .foxnews.com/story/0,2933,407003,00.html.

Chapter 4: The Drug Issue

39. Quoted in Fish. "Lost Legacy of the World's Fastest Man."

40. Quoted in Fish. "Lost Legacy of the World's Fastest Man."

41. Quoted in Matt Slater. "A Bolt for Athletics' Blues or Same Old Story?" BBC.co, June 2, 2008. www.bbc.co.uk/blogs/ olympics/2008/06/a_bolt_for_athletics_blues_or.html.

42. Quoted in Gary Gaffney. "New 100M World Record: Usain Bolt Sprints into Controversy." *Steroid Nation,* June 2, 2008. http://grg51.typepad.com/steroid_nation/2008/06/new-100m-world.html.

43. Quoted in Fish. "Lost Legacy of the World's Fastest Man."

44. Quoted in Kessel. "Olympics: Jamaican Speed Freak."

45. Quoted in Kessel. "Olympics: Jamaican Speed Freak."

46. Quoted in Duncan Mackay. "Profile of Victor Conte." Buzzle. com, December 4, 2004. www.buzzle.com/editorials/ 12-4-2004-62528.asp.

47. Gary Gaffney. "Why Is Usain Bolt Lightning Fast? Drugs, Doping, Genetics, Diet, Training, Slavery, or the Lack of NFL Scouts?" *Steroid Nation,* August 24, 2008. http://grg51

.typepad.com/steroid_nation/2008/08/why-is-usain-bo
.html.

48. Donald MacArthur. "The ACTN3 Sports Gene Test: What Can It Really Tell You?" *Genetic Future*, November 30, 2008. http://scienceblogs.com/geneticfuture/2008/11/the_actn3_ sports_gene_test_wha.php.

49. Quoted in Juliet Macur. "Born to Run: Little Ones Get Test for Sports Gene." *New York Times,* November 29, 2008, http://www.nytimes.com/2008/11/30/sports/30genetics .html?_r=1.

50. Quoted in Gaffney, "Why Is Usain Bolt Lightning Fast?"

51. Quoted in the Associated Press. "Ben Johnson Not Surprised by Marion Jones' Steroids Confession." ESPN.com, October 12, 2007. http://sports.espn.go.com/oly/news/ story?id=3060930.

Chapter 5: An Even Faster Year

52. Quoted in Sean Gregory. "#5 Usain Bolt (Person of the Year)." *Time*, December 28, 2009, p. 125.

53. Quoted in Christopher Clarey. "Bolt Shatters 100-Meter World Record." *New York Times,* August 16, 2009, p. D1.

54. Quoted in Lee West. "Usain Bolt Reveals How Horror Car Crash Made Him Change His Life." *Daily Mirror* (London), May 16, 2009. www.mirror.co.uk/sport/more-sport/2009/05/16/usain-bolt-reveals-how-horror-car-crash-made-im-change-his-life-115875-21364119/.

55. Quoted in David Powell. "2009 AF Golden League Review." IAAF.org, December 16, 2009. www.iaaf.org/GLE09/news/ newsid=55106.html.

56. Quoted in Powell. "2009 AF Golden League Review."

57. Quoted in Larry Rawson. "Bolt Lowers 100-Meter Mark to 9.58." ESPN Track and Field, August 16, 2009. http://sports .espn.go.com/oly/trackandfield/news/story?id=4402644.

58. Quoted in Clarey. "Bolt Shatters 100-Meter World Record."

59. Quoted in Rawson. "Bolt Lowers 100-Meter Mark to 9.58."

60. Quoted in *BBC Sport*. "Awesome Bolt Breaks 200M Record." BBC.co, August 20, 2009. http://news/bbc.co.uk/sport2/hi/ athletics/8213036.stm.

61. Quoted in Gregory. "#5 Usain Bolt (Person of the Year)."
62. Quoted in *BBC Sport.* "Awesome Bolt Breaks 200M Record."
63. Michael Johnson. "Why Usain Bolt Should Slow Down." *Newsweek International,* October 5, 2009, p. 14.
64. Johnson. "Why Usain Bolt Should Slow Down."

Chapter 6: 2010 and Beyond

65. Quoted in Fish. "Lost Legacy of the World's Fastest Man."
66. Quoted in Rojo Grande. "Usain Bolt's Next Challenge: 400 Meters." *Bleacher Report,* March 1, 2010. http://bleacher report.com/articles/354321-usain-bolts-next-challenge-400-meters.
67. Quoted in Leon Mann. "Johnson Suggests Bolt 400M Switch." *BBC Sport,* March 3, 2010. http://news.bbc.co.uk/go/pr/fr/-/sport2/hi/athletics/8557311.stm.
68. Quoted in Nick Harris. "The Greatest: Usain Bolt." *Independent* (London), August 22, 2009. www.independent.co.uk/news/people/profiles/the-greatest-usain-bolt-1775843.html.
69. Quoted in Harris. "The Greatest: Usain Bolt."
70. Quoted in Harris. "The Greatest: Usain Bolt."
71. Luke Dittrich. "Usain Bolt: Mutant." *Esquire,* April 2, 2010.
72. Quoted in Donald McRae. "Usain Bolt Warns the World's Sprinters That the Best Is Yet to Come." *Guardian* (Manchester, UK), March 30, 2010, p. 6.
73. Quoted in McRae. "Usain Bolt Warns the World's Sprinters That the Best Is Yet to Come."
74. Quoted in McRae. "Usain Bolt Warns the World's Sprinters That the Best Is Yet to Come."
75. Quoted in David Epstein. "Electrifying." *Sports Illustrated,* May 3, 2010. http://sportsillustrated.cnn.com/vault/article/magazine/MAG1168951/index.htm.
76. Quoted in Amy Shipley. "Usain Bolt Electrifies the Penn Relays." *Washington Post,* April 25, 2010. www.washingtonpost.com/wp-dyn/content/article/2010/04/24/AR2010042402456.html.
77. Quoted in Samuel Petrequin. "Usain Bolt Wins 100 Meters at Paris Diamond League." Associated Press, July 16, 2010. http://readingeagle.com/article.aspx?id=234682.

78. Quoted in Simon Briggs. "Usain Bolt Keeps Wary Eye on Golden Challengers Despite Taking Paris by Storm." *Daily Telegraph*, July 17, 2010. www.telegraph.co.uk/sport/other sports/athletics/7896458/Usain-Bolt-keeps-wary-eye-on-golden-challengers-despite-taking-Paris-by-storm.html.

79. Quoted in Chuck Schilken. "U.S. Sprinter Tyson Gay Beats 100-Meter World Record Holder Usain Bolt in Stockholm." *Los Angeles Times*, August 6, 2010. http://latimesblogs.latimes.com/sports_blog/2010/08/us-sprinter-tyson-gay-beats-100meter-world-record-holder-usain-bolt-in-stock-holm.html.

80. Quoted in IAAF Online Diaries. "After Back-to-Back 100M Victories, Bolt Relishing Brief Mid-Season Return to Jamaica." July 23, 2010. www.iaaf.org/athletes/diary/athl-code=184599/newsid=57588.html.

81. Usain Bolt. Facebook.com. July 22, 2010. www.facebook.com/usainbolt.

82. Quoted in Milton Kent. "Usain Bolt: Tyson Gay 'Probably Hates My Guts.'" *Fanhouse*, September 1, 2010. www.fanhouse.com/2010/09/01/usain-bolt-tyson-gay-probably-hates-my-guts/.

83. Quoted in McRae. "Usain Bolt Warns the World's Sprinters That the Best Is Yet to Come."

84. Quoted in Dittrich. "Usain Bolt: Mutant."

85. Quoted in Dittrich. "Usain Bolt: Mutant."

86. Quoted in McRae. "Usain Bolt Warns the World's Sprinters That the Best Is Yet to Come."

1986
Usain Bolt is born to Jennifer and Wellesley Bolt in Sherwood Content, Trelawny, Jamaica on August 21.

1999
Bolt enters high school at William Knibb Memorial High School, where his coach, Dwight Barnett, persuades him to take up track and field.

2001
Bolt takes second place at the annual high school championships and receives his first medal. Norman Peart becomes Bolt's manager.

In April Bolt wins silver medals in the two-hundred- and four-hundred-meter races at the CARIFTA (Caribbean Free Trade Association) Games in Barbados.

2002
The prime minister of Jamaica, P.J. Patterson, arranges for Bolt to move from Trelawny to Kingston to take advantage of the training facilities of the Jamaica Amateur Athletic Association.

Bolt wins gold medals in the two-hundred- and four-hundred-meter races at the CARIFTA Games in April.

In July Bolt wins a gold medal in the two-hundred-meter race at the IAAF (International Association of Athletics Federations) World Junior Championships in Kingston, Jamaica, at fifteen years old, the youngest runner to win gold. He also wins silver medals in the one-hundred-meter sprint and the four-hundred-meter relay.

2003
In July Bolt wins gold medals in the two-hundred-meter races at the IAAF World Youth Championships in Sherbrooke, Canada,

and the Pan-Am Junior Championships in Barbados. He also wins a silver medal in the four-hundred-meter race in Sherbrooke.

2004

Bolt turns professional under the guidance of coach Fitz Coleman.

Bolt wins the two-hundred-meter race at the CARIFTA games but suffers a hamstring injury in April.

Hampered by his hamstring injury, Bolt is eliminated in the first round of the two-hundred-meter run at the Summer Olympics in Athens, Greece, on August 24.

Glen Mills becomes Bolt's new coach in the fall.

2006

On September 17 Bolt places second in the two-hundred-meter race at the IAAF World Cup in Athens, Greece, and third in the two-hundred-meter race at the IAAF World Athletics Final in Stuttgart, Germany.

2007

Bolt wins the two-hundred-meter dash at the 2007 Jamaican Championships in June, breaking the thirty-six-year-old national record held by Dan Quarrie.

Bolt wins silver in the two-hundred-meter race as well as in relay races at the 2007 IAAF World Championships in Osaka, Japan.

2008

Bolt breaks Asafa Powell's world record in the hundred meters at the Reebok Grand Prix in New York City, earning his first world record on may 31.

Bolt wins three medals at the 2008 Summer Olympic Games in Beijing, setting world records in the one-hundred- and two-hundred-meter races and the four-hundred-meter relay.

2009

On April 29 Bolt suffers minor injuries in a car accident in St. Catherine, Jamaica. He was driving barefoot in a BMW M3 coupe that was a twenty-second-birthday gift from one of his sponsors.

Bolt wins three gold medals at the 2009 IAAF World Championships held in Berlin, Germany in August, breaking his previous records for the one-hundred- and two-hundred-meter races.

In November Bolt is named male winner of the IAAF World Athlete of the Year award.

2010

Bolt wins two Diamond League races—the hundred meters in South Korea and the two hundred meters in China in May.

Bolt announces that he has 2 million fans on his Facebook site.

Books

Usain Bolt. *Usain Bolt.* New York: HarperSport, 2010. A heavily illustrated autobiography of the runner and his Caribbean roots.

Alvin Campbell. *Usain Bolt: In the Fast Lane.* London: Arcadia, 2009. A biography of Bolt.

Periodicals

Rick Broadbent. "Usain Bolt: A Jamaican Miracle." *Times* (London), August 18, 2008. www.timesonline.co.uk/tol/sport/olympics/article4551396.ece.

Luke Dittrich. "Usain Bolt: Mutant." *Esquire,* April 2, 2010.

Mike Fish. "Lost Legacy of the World's Fastest Man." ESPN.com, August 13, 2009. http://sports.espn.go.com/oly/trackand field/columns/story?columnist=fish_mike&id=4395056.

Sean Gregory. "#5 Usain Bolt (Person of the Year)." *Time,* December 28, 2009.

Anna Kessel. "Olympics: Jamaican Speed Freak." *Observer* (London), August 24, 2008.

Anna Kessel. "Usain Bolt's Rise from Rags to Rapid Riches." *Observer* (London), August 9, 2009.

Tim Layden. "Bolt Strikes Twice." *Sports Illustrated,* August 31, 2009. http://sportsillustrated.cnn.com/vault/article/magazine/MAG1159481/index.htm.

Tim Layden. "The Phenom." *Sports Illustrated,* August 16, 2008. http://sportsillustrated.cnn.com.2008/writers/tim_layden/07/23/usain.bolt0728/.

Websites

IAAF.org: Home of World Athletics (www.iaaf.org/athletes/bio graphies/country=jam/athcode=185599.index.html). The site of the preeminent sports organization.

Usain Bolt (www.facebook.com/usainbolt). The official Facebook site about Usain Bolt. As of July 2010, more than 2 million fans are linked to this site, providing messages from Bolt along with links to news items and videos.

Usain Bolt (www.usainbolt.com). Usain Bolt's official website contains news stories, a biography, training advice to young racers, photographs and video clips, and a schedule of upcoming races.

Usain Bolt: The Runner (usainbolt.org). A weblog about Usain Bolt that contains articles and videos.

Among his thirty books and hundreds of newspaper columns on various subjects, George Cantor wrote ten books about sports topics that include the Olympics, the Detroit Tigers, University of Michigan football, and Paul Brown of the Cleveland Browns. Cantor was a Detroit-based journalist for more than forty years, serving as sportswriter and travel writer for the *Detroit Free Press*, columnist and editorial page writer for the *Detroit News*, and columnist for the *Jewish News*. He was the commentator of a radio program, "More Than the Music," for several years and often was called upon to discuss sports and other topics on Detroit radio and television programs. Cantor received a lifetime achievement award from the Society of Professional Journalists in April 2010 and, shortly after his death in August 2010, was inducted into the Jewish Sports Hall of Fame.